3.49

Published by SuperSummary, www.supersummary.com

ISBN: 9798419123861

For more information or to learn about our complete library of study guides, please visit http://www.supersummary.com.

Please submit comments or questions to: http://www.supersummary.com/support/

Table of Contents

Overview

The Uses of Enchantment: The Meaning and Importance of Fairy Tales (1976) won acclaims such as the US National Book Award and the National Book of Critics Circle Award. Its author, Bruno Bettelheim (1903-1990), was an Austrian-born psychoanalyst and public intellectual who worked primarily in the United States. Bettelheim wrote *The Uses of Enchantment* to persuade parents and educators that the European fairy tale, with all its fantastical and violent content, was a greater aid to child development than the more anodyne realistic contemporary children's literature: While the latter type of literature might reflect a child's everyday experiences, the fairy tale is more truthful in its presentation of a child's chaotic inner life and more consoling in its suggestions of creative solutions.

In his *New York Times* review of Bettelheim's book, John Updike explains how Bettelheim drew upon the work of Sigmund Freud and Carl Jung, who used fairy tales to explain psychoanalytic motifs: "[W]hat is new, and exciting, is the warmth, humane and urgent, with which Bettelheim expounds fairy tales as aids to the child's growth [...] Bettelheim's readings make sense of much that seems nonsensical" (Updike, John. "The Uses of Enchantment." *The New York Times*. 1976). However, Updike speculates that the fairy tales discussed in Bettelheim's book are "medieval in spirit as well as setting, and saturated in Christian cosmology"; he is skeptical of the fairy tales' universality and posits that decontextualizing the stories risks misunderstanding their full significance.

Indeed, leading fairy tale scholars American Jack Zipes and British Marina Warner both acknowledge Bettelheim's academic importance but argue that his scholarship is patchy and incomplete, and, decades after the book's publication, Bettelheim's reputation suffered a downturn. In a 1991 article titled "Bruno Bettelheim's Uses of Enchantment and Abuses of Scholarship," UC Berkeley anthropologist Alan Dundes demonstrates how Bettelheim plagiarized Julius Heuscher's 1963 work *A Psychiatric Study of Myths and Fairy Tales: Their Origin, Meaning, and Usefulness* alongside other texts. This has destroyed the myth of the originality of Bettelheim's arguments and undermined his scholarly authority.

This guide uses the 1991 British Penguin Edition.

Summary

The Uses of Enchantment begins with Bettelheim's argument that fairy tales are far more useful than contemporary realistic children's literature in helping a child find meaning in themselves and the world. He emphasizes that literature must meet the child at their stage in development rather than prematurely trying to impose a rational, adult view on them. The fairy tale, with its violent and fantastic scenes, parallels the child's inner turmoil. At the same time, it encourages the child to identify with noble but relatable protagonists to psychologically access the next developmental stage and work towards their own happy conclusion.

In studies of famous, largely European fairy tales, Bettelheim argues that the stories' components encourage children at different developmental stages to find a more mature, independent approach to the world. For example, the author asserts, some fairy tales' polarizing dual parental personas—the original, dead good mother versus the demanding, withholding stepmother—enables the child to hold onto the supportive image of a nurturer who loves them and believes in their future, even as they seek to defeat and surpass the woman who inhibits them. Bettelheim argues that fairy tales negotiate the oedipal drama of the child's wish to destroy the same-sex parent in order to be first with the opposite-sex parent. Here, the stories employ symbols and images to show children that they recognize their predicament and then offer healthier alternatives to their immature, destructive wishes. Bettelheim also claims that fairy tales can help the reader achieve psychoanalytic personality integration, where the animalistic id is given full rein before it is brought under the control of the superego and ego. In the animal groom cycle of tales, where a heroine gives up her repression of sexuality in order to have a happy marriage, Bettelheim says that love is the means through which the violent, antisocial aspects of the id can be redeemed. Thus, what seemed dangerous and uncontrollable is revealed for its true beauty and naturalness.

Bettelheim believes the best fairy tales promote a happy ending and that they show how, after overcoming serious obstacles, the hero can look forward to a future of autonomy from their parents and a union with an opposite-sex partner onto whom they can healthily transfer their earlier oedipal attachment (the "Oedipus complex" is a radically heteronormative Freudian concept of psychosexual development, and the author centers this concept throughout the text). Bettelheim posits that all tales are relevant to different types of children, regardless of their age or gender. Thus, the child would derive meaning from the tale according to their circumstances and stage of development. He advocates repeated exposure to the same tale so that its motifs have the maximum opportunity to developmentally aid the child's unconscious.

Chapter Summaries & Analyses

Introduction

Introduction Summary: "The Struggle for Meaning"

Bettelheim argues that meaning and meaning-making—that is, making sense of one's experiences—is fundamental to human happiness and the ability to cope with adversity. Parents cannot impose their own sense of meaning on a child; rather, the child must find it itself and at their own pace. Bettelheim believes self-understanding is the most essential step towards meaning: By understanding oneself, one can progress to understanding others and forming relationships with them.

Writing as a psychoanalytic therapist to troubled children in the 1970s, Bettelheim believes that his duty is to restore a sense of meaning to their lives. He finds that many modern children's books do not help him in this endeavor, as they do not prepare children sufficiently for problems in the real world. These books share the dominant cultural view that young children should be offered a sanitized version of the world, where harsh realities—such as death, aging, and the worst aspects of human behavior—are removed. The problem with this is that "children know that *they* are not always good; and often, even when they are, they would prefer not to be" (7). Thus, the censored characters in modern children's literature contradict what children know to be true about themselves, and this makes the child "a monster in his own eyes" (7).

In contrast, says Bettelheim, fairy tales written and retold prior to the 20th century are better equipped to help a child deal with their turbulent feelings. These stories, which feature polarities of good and evil and show their young protagonists encountering the worst of human behavior, take seriously the most frightening parts of life while providing an optimistic view of a child's ability to face such challenges. From a psychoanalytic perspective, these tales encourage ego development: They relieve unconscious pressures by giving license to the id and showing how these shadowy parts can be brought into alignment with the expectations of the ego and superego. Importantly, the fairy tale, like psychoanalytic therapy, enables the child to accept the inevitable obstacles of life without being defeated by them.

While evil characters pervade fairy tales, these tales guide the reader toward morality by having them identify with the hero. Importantly, Bettelheim emphasizes that a child's moral behavior is predicated not on an altruistic impulse towards good but on a desire to resemble the hero. Similarly, these tales deal with universal fears, such as a fear of death, by offering the consolation of a lifelong bond to another. With such a happy ending, the fact of one's eventual death seems irrelevant.

The "future-orientated" nature of the fairy tale negotiates the other universal in childhood development—separation anxiety and the unconscious wish to hold onto one's mother eternally (11). Tales such as *Hansel and Gretel* show how those who aim to continue to depend on their parents are forced to change as they embark on the journey towards satisfying independence and peer bonds. Bettelheim argues that the changes in lifestyle between the time of fairy tales and the late 20th century are almost irrelevant, as the developmental problems children face are the same, especially regarding the sense of isolation present in childhood. Just as fairy tale heroes act alone, Bettelheim envisages a modern, city-dwelling child separated from their extended family and looking for meaning and rewarding interactions with the surrounding world.

Bettelheim writes the book to bring awareness to the importance of fairy tales. He argues that fairy tales are great works of art, and like all such works, each tale will meet each reader differently depending on their state of development. Rather than prescribing tales to their children and dictating what they should find significant, parents should instead allow their child to make their own journey through the stories, accepting that the child is finding motifs that support their development in the present moment.

Although Bettelheim urges parents to seek out the most original version of the fairy tale, he contradicts himself by saying the exact origins of the tales are obscure. He stresses that while most fairy tales have been lost, he will focus on the most popular and enduring ones.

Introduction Analysis

In his introduction, Bettelheim posits that fairy tales—those old-fashioned stories of hamlets and evil queens, which emerged from an oral-tradition —are a better companion to a growing child than contemporary realist children's literature. By the time Bettelheim was writing in the 1970s, the baby boomer generation of children was growing up in relative prosperity and stability. For privileged white, middle-class families especially, childhood came to be viewed as a hallowed time that needed protection from the full-scale horrors in the adult world. Contemporary children's literature reflected this attitude, refraining from dealing with the harshest parts of human experience and neglecting the primitive fears of violence that plague so many children.

Ironically, while the scenarios presented in modern realist texts may ring true to life, they give a vastly incomplete picture of a child's internal world and thus provide children with inadequate tools to cope with a world and a self they know to be far from benign. Bettelheim argues that parents who "want their children's minds to function as their own do" (3), and who seek an express ticket to their children's maturation, are uncomfortable with the dark, fantastical content of fairy tales because these parents do not appreciate that their children must undergo developmental tribulations for themselves. While the modern works function as consolation texts—arguably even to the parents—for an imperfect childhood, fairy tales address the true turmoil of separating from one's parents and becoming autonomous.

Further, Bettelheim parallels postwar, post-Vietnam American society's misunderstanding of fairy tales to their misunderstanding of psychoanalysis. Guided by the national veneration of the American dream, which states that any wish is possible with enough hard work, Americans want to use psychoanalysis to improve their lives, whereas Bettelheim stipulates that psychoanalysis' purpose is to help people understand life and cope with it. In fairy tales, the id—the animalistic, unconscious part of the personality—is given free rein through characters such as devouring giants and envious mothers. However, the id is ultimately controlled by the hero who acquires increasing ego strength as the story progresses. Through the hero, the child can find some sort of "American dream" trajectory, as they wishfully identify with the hero and are motivated to reach the next stage of psychological development. Bettelheim emphasizes that good identification with a hero character is a better motivator for maturation than pure altruism. In specifying this, Bettelheim encourages parents to accept that their children are reward-focused and even selfish (as a parent might otherwise hold onto idealistic views of their child's character).

Bettelheim was writing during the peak years of the American feminist movement, and his work gestures towards abandoning stereotypes when he says that children will identify with fairy tale protagonists regardless of their assigned gender. However, his continual use of the masculine pronoun "he" suggests the default child he refers to is male; a fact that diminishes female experience, even when Bettelheim applies his insights to children of either gender. While an earlier generation of readers may have been in the habit of regarding references to a male subject as a default for all humanity, modern audiences may find this problematic. Nonbinary readers especially may question the authority of a writer who not only does not acknowledge but erases them. Bettelheim also shows he is a product of his time in targeting a white, middle-class American audience with a Eurocentric background. This is evident when he assumes that his audience's familiarity with the same European fairy tales of the German Grimm Brothers, like *Hansel and Gretel,* and does takes no time to elaborate on the stories' origins.

Part 1

Part 1 Summary: "A Pocketful of Magic"

Life Divined from the Inside

Bettelheim argues that in fairy tales, "internal processes are externalized and comprehensible" (25). He recalls a tradition in Hindu medicine where a patient is given a fairy tale to meditate on when faced with a problem. While his external problems will be different from the fairy tale protagonist's, his internal conflict will be similar. Importantly, the fairy tale does not dictate the solution; rather, the meditator uses the tale as a guide to find his own solution and so is active in the model of his own healing.

Bettelheim continues to emphasize the role of fairy tales in "achieving a more mature consciousness to civilize the chaotic pressures of their unconscious" (24). These stories have evolved over generations to address universal concerns and provide the reassuring message that a good life is possible as long as we do not evade the struggles that push our current, limited identity toward a more mature and satisfying one. Bettelheim emphasizes that reading the story aloud to a child is the most helpful method of disseminating it as the parent thus affirms the child's process of using fairy tales as a guide to overcoming obstacles.

"The Fisherman and the Jinny": Fairy Tale Compared to Fable

"The Fisherman and the Jinny" is a tale from *The Arabian Nights*. In the story, a poor fisherman casts his net into the sea four times. The first three catches are futile, but the last brings a copper jar containing a giant Jinny (genie). The Jinny threatens to kill the fisherman, who saves himself by outwitting the Jinny: He teases the Jinny that he does not believe that a creature of such enormous size could fit into a container as small as the copper jar. When the Jinny re-enters the jar to challenge the fisherman's taunt, the fisherman quickly caps it and tosses it back into the ocean.

For Bettelheim, the Jinny's wrath compares to that of a young child when they feel deserted by their parents or caretakers. While a child first thinks of a happy reunion with their absent parent, after a time, the child will begin fantasizing about the revenge they will wreak on their abandoner. The trapped Jinny represents the "bottled-up feelings" of an abandoned child (30). Bettelheim emphasizes that "on his own, the child does not know what has happened to him—all he knows is that he has to act this way" (30). The idea that the child may be overpowered by their emotions is too intimidating a thought to harbor. With the introduction of the fairy tale, the child can unconsciously identify with the Jinny and process their frustration.

Another important feature of this tale is that the fisherman's net brings back nothing worthwhile until the fourth attempt. This provides the message that one must not give up even in the face of a few failures. In psychoanalysis, this relates to the triumph of the reality principle over the pleasure principle: While the drive for pleasure strives for immediate satisfaction and minimum discomfort, the reality principle engenders the ability to tolerate frustration with the hope of gaining an enduring reward.

Bettelheim shows that while myth and fable present the choice between pleasure and reality as didactic and allegorical, the fairy tale works more by implication and entices the young reader towards the more rewarding outcome rather than dictating to them.

Fairy Tale Versus Myth: Optimism Versus Pessimism

Bettelheim believes that fairy tales are more useful than myths in childhood development. Both these narrative types became part of the collective consciousness after being developed over centuries. Psychoanalysts agree that their symbols represent the content of our unconscious minds and convey messages for how to attain a higher state of selfhood. However, the difference between them is that while myth posits exemplary settings and specimens of humanity alongside awe-inspiring feats of heroism, the fairy tale presents the supernatural as "ordinary, something that could happen to you or me [...] when out on a walk in the woods" (37). The heroes and heroines are often little-described everyday folk with whom children can easily identify. The stories' diction emphasizes this by being casual as opposed to grandiose.

Bettelheim says myths can intimidate young children because they "project an ideal personality acting on the basis of superego demands" (41), thus giving the impression that no mere mortal could live up to such heroism and would be defeated. In contrast, fairy tales "depict an ego integration which allows for appropriate satisfaction of id desires" (41), as the child feels they can emulate the protagonists' actions in order to mature and find happiness.

He also argues that the tragic endings of myths are discouraging for youngsters, while fairy tales are optimistic because they generally provide the reassurance of a happy ending. Thus, the child is willing to empathetically undergo trials with the hero, safe in the knowledge that everything will be okay in the end.

"The Three Little Pigs": Pleasure Principle Versus Reality Principle

For Bettelheim, the fairy tale of the three little pigs is the best illustration of the pleasure principle's evolution into the reality principle. The three houses built by the pigs—made successively from straw, wood, and brick—represent humanity's progress throughout history, while the pigs' actions show "progress from the id-dominated personality to the superego-influenced but essentially ego-controlled personality" (42). The third pig, who builds his house from bricks, is the only one who has learned to subjugate his desire for play in order to work towards building a secure future in line with the reality principle. Thus, his efforts are the only match for the huffing and puffing wolf, who is an externalization of everything asocial and dangerous within people and society.

"The Three Little Pigs," says Bettelheim, is more useful than Aesop's fable of "The Ant and the Grasshopper," which has a similar moral about the need to be industrious and sacrifice pleasure to prepare for the future. In this fable, the hard-working ant punishes the grasshopper—who sang instead of working during the summer—by refusing to share his food store come winter. Such a fable forces the child to identify with the priggish, mean-spirited ant, whereas the three little pigs represent different stages within psychic development. It is not too traumatic for the child that the first two pigs get eaten by the wolf as "the child understands subconsciously that we have to shed earlier forms of existence if we wish to move on to higher ones" (44).

The Child's Need for Magic

Bettelheim stipulates that regardless of our age, "only a story conforming to the principles underlying our thought processes carries conviction for us" (45). Thus, with a child who is animalistic in their thinking and sees the entire world as made up of animate components, they will be better helped to contemplate life's eternal questions—such as identity or the purpose of life—by fairy tales; fairy tales imitate the child's "underlying thought process" (45) because they are populated with animate being, such as talking animals and dolls, rather than rational explanations. While many parents may dismiss the fantastical and try to rush their children's integration into the rational world, this may backfire because children lack the abstract thought required for such rationality. In their hurry to provide scientific explanations, such parents ignore scientific findings about how a child's mind works. Instead, a child will be better prepared for the rational world and the truth about their miniscule place in the cosmos if they are made to feel secure. The child derives "security only from the conviction that he understands now what baffled him before—never from being given facts which create *new* uncertainties" (48). Bettelheim even says that teens who experiment with drugs or seek salvation at the hands of some guru were often given an insufficient exposure to magic in their childhoods. Having missed out on this significant formative experience, they now seek other means to find "magical" security.

While some parents introduce biblical or religious stories instead of fairy tales, children struggle with this material as they do not see the dark side of their nature reflected in the examples of sainthood. Similarly, says Bettelheim, in their extreme moralistic view, these biblical stories do not allow a child to feel and progress through their negative emotions. As a result, these biblical stories are not as useful as fairy tales.

Vicarious Satisfaction Versus Conscious Recognition

Fairy tales are uniquely equipped to enable a child "to bring some order into the inner chaos of his mind so that he can understand himself better —a necessary preliminary for achieving some congruence between his perceptions and the external world" (53).

Prior to school age, a child's great struggle is to prevent their desires from taking over and overwhelming their whole personality. The child is ruled by the appetites of the id—unconscious drives that they feel that they can little control. As the child grows, the id, ego, and superego become more distinct, and the child will be able to interact with the unconscious without it overpowering the conscious mind and without feeling that they have lost mastery over themselves. Fairy tales, even more than self-invented fantasies, can help this development, as they model how to externalize difficult feelings. After reading, the child can practice the lessons of the fairy tale through play. Bettelheim strongly advocates that the child should be allowed to experiment freely and unselfconsciously without the parent explaining the psychological workings that are going on as the child experiences the tale. To do so would take away the enjoyment and overwhelm the child who may be unable to bear hearing exactly what id-related desires they are channeling as they experience the tale.

As the fairy tale does not directly relate to the child and their immediate experiences, but someone like them, they feel more comfortable discussing its issues. Repeated readings are key, as it can take time for the full effects of the tale to absorb. This can only happen when the child is able to linger over a tale's meaning or relate to a protagonist who seems unlike them. Thus, "for the fairy tale to have beneficial externalization effects, the child must remain unaware of the unconscious pressures he is responding to by making fairy-story solutions of his own" (58). For this reason, too, Bettelheim recommends unillustrated versions of fairy tales as illustrations supplement the artist's vision and make the story less personal and therefore less powerful.

The Importance of Externalization: Fantasy Figures and Events

Fantasy is an essential component of filling in the gaps in a child's understanding, but unless they find a way of ordering such fantasies, a child may become weakened or confused by them. Fairy tales can give clarity to such fantasies by bringing up a child's conflict in an alternative form and offering the opportunity to externalize inner experience. Figures such as witches can embody unmanageable traits such as destructive wishes, as the child begins the process of sorting out his contradictions.

The vagueness at the beginning of fairy tales that take place in distant times and lands "suggest[s] a voyage into the interior of our mind, into the realms of unawareness and the unconscious" (63). The fairy tale accompanies the child into this terrain, but does not get lost there, as its structure ensures that the hero progresses through the land of magic back to reality.

By sharing fairy tales with their children, parents pass on the message that they consider their children's "inner experiences as embodied in fairy tales worthwhile, legitimate, and in some fashion even 'real'" (64). . Parents' validation of their children's feelings gives the children the sense that they are important to their parents. In contrast, if children are only told stories that are true to life, which ignore their fantasy-filled inner lives, they may believe that their feelings and, by extension, they themselves, are unimportant to their parents.

Transformations: The Fantasy of the Wicked Stepmother

Fairy tales play an essential role in helping the child bridge the gap between their internal experiences and the real world. Bettelheim asserts that this is evident in the fantasy of the wicked stepmother, an envious, pleasure-denying imposter figure found in many fairy tales who takes the place of the child's adoring original mother. In real life, when the child's mother denies their needs or wishes, the child creates two figures in their head, as the mother changes from "all-giving protector" to "cruel stepmother" (67). This splitting of the mother into two personae allows the child to keep the image of the good, generous mother "uncontaminated," which is essential to their sense of security (67). The stepmother figure also becomes a scapegoat for the child's anger, which does not need to tarnish the real, good mother. Bettelheim claims that such splitting also takes place in many young children's fantasy where they are adopted and end up cohabiting with their denying, demanding stepparents by mistake, while their noble, good parents are elsewhere.

Further, says Bettelheim, the child also splits themselves into good and bad figures. Bettelheim recalls that nighttime bedwetters often create an alias for the person who wet their bed, thus disidentifying with this transgressive part of themselves. Because it is too frightening for the child to view that their conscious self is responsible for this accident, it feels safer to place the blame onto someone else altogether. Bettelheim views that insisting to the child that they take ownership of the bedwetting will cause shame and delay the integration of their personality. Instead, parents should allow the bedwetting phase to pass and for the child to achieve a self that they can be proud of. Then, with time, the child will be able to accept that they can be flawed without being a bad person.

Bringing Order into Chaos

Bettelheim says that before and during the oedipal period, when the child is between three and six, their internal world is chaotic and confused. The child is often overwhelmed by extreme emotions that hit upon the opposites of love and hate, good and bad, because they "cannot comprehend intermediate stages of degree and intensity" (74). Fairy tales offer a parallel world for this inner experience, owing to the polarities of its figures, who are entirely good and helpful or destructive and devouring. The child can use the fairy tale to create a system that "suggests not only isolating and separating the disparate and confusing aspects of the child's experience into opposites, but projecting these onto different figures" (75).

These extremes of good and bad are not unlike the distinct aspects of the personality conceived of by Freud: the superego, ego and id. Like the figures in the fairy tale, these separations are also fictions and only useful for sorting out our tangled thoughts. In fairy tales, the id is often symbolized in animals. Like the wolf in "The Little Red Riding Hood," it is an entirely destructive force. However, when shaped by the ego and superego, the animalistic id represents our physical energy and is part of an integrated personality.

"The Queen Bee": Achieving Integration

Bettelheim considers the Grimm brothers' little-known story "The Queen Bee" to be the best illustration of the id's integration with the superego and ego. It relates the story of a king's three sons. The oldest two boys are given up to a wanton existence dominated by the id. The youngest son, Simpleton, goes out to join them. Guided by the nobler values of the superego and ego, Simpleton insists that the older brothers should not disturb the ants, ducks, or bees they encounter on the road. They arrive at the castle of another king where everything has been turned to stone. A little gray man submits the oldest brother to the challenge of gathering a thousand pearls that are hidden in the moss of the forest. When he fails, he is punished by being turned to stone. The same fate meets the second brother.

Simpleton is also daunted by this task, however, the ants he has saved from his brother's malice come to his rescue. When it comes to performing two subsequently challenging tasks, the ducks and queen bee he has saved help him. He is rewarded with marriage to the castle's youngest and most loveable princess and inheriting the kingdom.

For Bettelheim, the two eldest brothers "who were unresponsive to the requirements of personality integration failed to meet the tasks of reality" (77). Their petrification symbolizes their being asleep to everything except the appetites of the id. Simpleton, who is influenced by the ego and superego, is also incapable of meeting the grounds of reality in the story. However, when his animal nature, symbolic of the id, "has been befriended, recognized as important, and brought into accord with ego and superego" (78), he achieves the total personality to complete the tasks. His self-mastery is symbolized by the reward of kingship.

"Brother and Sister": Unifying Our Dual Nature

Bettelheim argues that prior to achieving personality integration, our superego and id "war against each other" (78). The child is aware of such a duality when he wants to obey his mother's order to not eat a cookie while also wanting to eat the cookie. Fairy tales can aid the understanding of such inner conflict.

The Brothers Grimm tale "Brother and Sister" puts these two rival instincts into two separate personae. When a brother and sister leave home in search of a better life, the sister is better able to control her desire to drink as she listens to the murmuring of water telling her she will be turned into a different animal each time if she does. While she twice restrains her more id-driven brother, the third time he succumbs to his thirst and is turned into a fawn. The sister places her golden garter around his neck—a gesture that, for Bettelheim, symbolizes forgoing a purely animal nature for a higher state of humanity.

The sister and fawn make a life in the forest. However, one day, the fawn demands to be let out so it can enjoy the excitement of the king's hunt, despite the risk to its life. The king notices the golden garter around the fawn's neck and asks that it should be captured but not killed. When the fawn is found at the hut, alongside the girl, the king finds the girl beautiful and asks her to marry him. They live happily alongside the fawn.

However, when the girl, now a queen, gives birth to a son, a witch poses as a lady in waiting and suffocates the queen, placing her own daughter in the queen's bed. The queen, however, returns nightly (and presumably in some spiritual form) to tend to her child and her brother fawn. A nursemaid witnesses this and tells the king, who calls the queen his "beloved wife" and so brings her back to life (82). Later, when the witch is found and brought to justice, the fawn regains his human form. For Bettelheim, the story shows the triumph of human qualities over animalistic ones, as the integration of the superego and id can only happen when injustice, in the form of the witch, has been done away with. He adds that the transitions of moving away from the parental home and childbirth are significant for the brother's animal transformation and the sister's death, because they represent crisis points where one way of living must be exchanged for another. In the end, the sister's superego-driven concern for others redeems both her and her more id-driven brother.

"Sinbad the Seaman and Sinbad the Porter": Fancy Versus Reality

This tale from *The Arabian Nights* features a poor porter called Sinbad listening to the intrepid escapades of a rich voyager. Symbolically, we are made to understand that the porter and traveler are "the same person in different forms" as the voyager addresses the porter as his brother and the porter wonders what it would be like to be the voyager (84). For Bettelheim, the porter's longing for the voyager's life occurs when "the ego, exhausted by its tasks, then permits itself to be overwhelmed by the id" (85). The voyager's life of pleasure is more in line with the id. However, this only happens at the level of thought, as the porter returns to a state of ego-dominance and his duty-filled life.

Bettelheim admires the story for making both the voyager and the porter attractive characters and so giving the message that all sides of our personality are equally valid. Still, he wishes that there were a happy ending to the story, with the two living together in a manner that symbolizes psychic integration.

The Frame Story of *Thousand and One Nights*

In the frame story (overarching narrative that contains multiple shorter stories) of the *Thousand and One Nights*, King Shahryar discovers his wife has betrayed him with one of his slaves and, losing all trust in humanity, he becomes dominated by his id. The disappointments he has endured means that his ego can no longer restrain his id; he therefore forcibly sleeps with a different "nubile virgin" every night before killing her in the morning and moving onto the next. The vizier's daughter Scheherazade wishes to be the king's "means of deliverance" by telling the king a different fairy tale every night (87). On each occasion, he spares her life by giving her the chance to live another day and tell a different tale. In Bettelheim's view, the multiplicity of Scheherazade's tales represents how no single story can ever provide a solution to all our problems.

The author regards Scheherazade as having "a superego-dominated ego which has become so cut off from selfish id that it is ready to risk the person's very existence to obey a moral obligation" (88). However, the king is only redeemed when Scheherazade begins to love him, drawing upon the id's positive energies for her constructive purposes. They thus achieve integration, the only state that prevents humanity from being riven in two by contradictory impulses.

Tales of Two Brothers

Tales that feature two brothers of opposing personalities are at least as old as the example found on an Egyptian papyrus of 1250 BC. Bettelheim counts at least 770 different versions of a tale where one brother seeks an adventurous life dominated by the id, while another is more cautious and wishes to stay at home. For Bettelheim, these opposing figures represent a dichotomy inherent within each of us: "the striving for independence and self-assertion, and the opposite tendency to remain safely at home, tied to the parents" (91). The latter brother may be laboring under an oedipal attachment, whereby if he fails to differentiate himself from his parents, he will be destroyed. The stories assert that we cannot thrive without an integration of both tendencies, as the two brothers set off on a journey of discovery and self-realization.

Interestingly, Bettelheim asserts that a key motivator for going on the journey is the hope that we will re-encounter "the all-giving mother of our infancy" in another form, even as we trick ourselves into believing we seek an autonomous existence (94).

"The Three Languages": Building Integration

This Brothers' Grimm story tells the tale of an adolescent who fails his father's demands to learn from three esteemed masters and is cast out. While his father demands that his servants kill the boy, the servants take pity on him and leave him out in the woods. Bettelheim argues that after ignoring the father's demands and surviving anyway, the boy worries that the father will seek to retaliate by destroying him.

He sets out on his own path, stubbornly insisting on learning "what he thinks is of real value" (100). He learns the language of birds, dogs, and frogs, with the frogs prophesying a future that he will become Pope. He achieves this, owing to the integration of his personality.

"The Three Feathers": The Youngest Child as Simpleton

The number three appears often in fairy tales. In psychoanalysis, the number can stand for the ego, superego, and id. However, in the Brothers Grimm's tale *The Three Feathers*, it pertains to how the youngest and "simplest" brother, who is still aligned with the instinctive nature of his unconscious, triumphs over the other two.

Fairy tales that show the triumph of youngest children are immensely comforting to small children who can feel inferior and insignificant compared to the larger parents and siblings who seem to know so much more. These stories offer the message that the child is fine as they are and that they can develop into someone capable of a happy ending.

The number three is especially pertinent for young children because "in the child's mind, 'two' stands usually for the two parents, and 'three' for the child himself in relation to his parents, but not to his siblings" (106). However, as it is too intimidating to think about wanting to overcome one's parents, the fairy tale transfigures the parental duo into older siblings, with whom the child is in conscious rivalry. In "The Three Feathers," a father challenges his three sons to follow the direction of the feathers he blows into the air to find him the finest carpet. The two eldest sons, who consider themselves clever, follow their feathers to far-flung destinations east and west, but the youngest brother's feather falls to the earth. While this originally seems inauspicious, it leads to a trapdoor and an underground realm of discovery. To Bettelheim, this trapdoor represents the unconscious, the instinctual part of our personality that gives us the bulk of our strength. The two elder brothers are undifferentiated from each other and un-special, because they function on "the basis of a much-depleted ego [...] cut off from the potential of its strength and riches, the id" (108). This prevents them from growing, unlike the youngest brother, who is guided by instinct to make wise choices and excel. This provides hope to young children, who are less sophisticated but often more instinctual than their learned parents.

Oedipal Conflicts and Resolutions: The Knight in Shining Armor and the Damsel in Distress

Drawing on the emphatically heteronormative Freudian concept of the Oedipus complex (as he does consistently throughout the text), Bettelheim maintains that a little boy in the throes of oedipal conflict wants his mother to cherish him above all others and seeks to get his father out of the way. However, the boy worries about what his much more powerful father would do to him if he found out. The fairy tale, says Bettelheim, provides a solution to this problem by pretending that it is not a father-figure but rather an evil dragon who prevents one from having one's mother for oneself: This story "gives veracity to the boy's feeling that the most desirable female is kept in captivity by an evil figure, while implying that it is not Mother the child wants for himself, but a marvelous and wonderful woman he hasn't met yet, but certainly will"

(111).

Bettelheim then describes theoretical oedipal little girl, who resents her mother's hold over her father but at the same time needs her mother's care to survive; in this case, says the author, stories about an evil stepmother who keeps her captive and away from her prince fulfill the function of seeing herself as desirable enough for a prince-like figure and also as a person that a denying mother would be jealous of and threatened by. There is also a pre-oedipal good mother, who would have granted the girl's every wish and never prevented her union with the prince (the stand-in for father). For the girl, "belief and trust in the goodness of the pre-oedipal mother, and deep loyalty to her, tend to reduce the guilt about what the girl wishes would happen to the (step)mother who stands in her way" (114).

The author believes that such fantasies, which are condoned by parents who read their children fairy tales, can help with the resolution of oedipal conflicts.

Fear of Fantasy: Why Were Fairy Tales Outlawed?

Bettelheim argues that it is irrational for adults to outlaw fairy tales in the belief they are harmful. Some parents object to fairy tales because they fear lying to their children owing to the make-believe world the tales present. However, children have different understandings of truth and want to be assured that the stories they are told address their most pressing concerns.

Rather than obstructing a child's ability to cope with reality, fairy tales and the rich fantasy life they engender help, as an ability to imagine fantastical phenomena gives "the ego an abundance of material to work with" and stops it being trapped in narratives of wish-fulfillment (119).

The fairy tale's detractors fear the grim content of fairy tales and the fact that witches and giants may be stand-in figures for parents; they instead give their children stories where the id is repressed. This attempt to deplete the unconscious is counterproductive, as the unconscious nurtures the ego. Moreover, watered-down storybook villains make the child feel truly alone with the most "monstrous" parts of their nature, whereas fairy tales show that even their most difficult feelings are normal and shared by others.

Transcending Infancy with the Help of Fantasy

A rich fantasy life can aid the transition from infancy to childhood, as the child moves away from their unrealistic expectations of being the receptacle of their parents' unceasing gifts in favor of self-sufficiency. As the child grows up, they can feel the pressure of parental expectation in addition to disillusionment following their shortcomings. An ability to fantasize about a better future in which one has more influence and empowerment can help a child to cope and attain the next stage of development. Fairy tales can guide children to imagine their own futures optimistically. For example, a child may be dispossessed of the endlessly giving parents of their infancy whilst still living under the frustration of being dominated by them, but the child can use the fairy tale to imagine their own kingdom, a place where they are rulers of themselves. The fairy tale aids them to imagine the coming-of-age challenges they must face before ascending to such a privilege. Bettelheim explains, "[W]hile the fantasy is *unreal*, the good feelings it gives us about ourselves and our future *are real*, and these real good feelings are what we need to sustain us" (126).

Fairy tale fantasies can aid children with negotiating their problems. Bettelheim compares the fairy tale of "Rapunzel" to the more anodyne modern text of *The Swiss Family Robinson*, finding the latter text deficient in providing no witch figure onto which a girl can transfer her feelings towards a troubling maternal figure.

"The Goose Girl": Achieving Autonomy

Bettelheim recounts another fairy tale: An old queen sends her beautiful daughter to a foreign land to be married. She is accompanied by her talking horse, Falada, and an attendant maid, and she takes a handkerchief with three spots of her mother's blood on it.

On the journey, the maid says that she refuses to be the girl's servant, and when the girl stops to drink at a stream, she loses her mother's handkerchief with the blood and becomes weak. The maid takes advantage of her weakness and forces them to swap dresses; the maid now masquerades as the princess. She becomes the young king's betrothed and chops off Falada's head for the fear that the talking horse will give her away. Meanwhile, the true princess is employed as a lowly goose girl, helping a boy tend geese. When the old king asks the goose girl her story, she says she is bound by a vow to not tell anyone. However, she will tell it to the hearth, and the old king listens. After this, she receives royal garments and marries the young king. Under the pretense of seeking counsel, the old king asks the pretending maid (or false princess) to describe a punishment for an interloper, and she says that such a person should be put in a nail studded barrel and dragged up and down the street by two horses until she is dead. The old king proclaims that she, the maid, is the interloper and will be punished according to her own specification.

Bettelheim uses this story to illustrate his claim that the theme of a pretender usurping the hero's place helps the child negotiate the oedipal conflict. At first, the child thinks the pretender is the same-sex parent who is keeping them from a union with the opposite-sex parent. Then, as they mature, the child will recognize themselves as the pretender who wants to take the same-sex parent's rightful place. According to Bettelheim, the child learns from the story that it is safer to accept the maid's childish impotent position than to usurp the place of a parent.

The next lesson is that the handkerchief spotted with blood symbolizes sexual maturity. By losing the handkerchief, the princess delays ascendance into maturity and being usurped as she is forced to take the childish, disempowered position of goose girl. She has been too weak and passive in succumbing to the maid, and it is not until she is able to mature and develop her own personality that a happy ending is possible. While adults worry that the punishments to evil figures such as the imposter maid disturb young children, Bettelheim resolves that "final success is experienced as meaningless by the child if his underlying unconscious anxieties are not also resolved" (141). Thus, the fairy tale must conclude with the destruction of the evil doer.

Fantasy, Recovery, Escape, and Consolation

Bettelheim cites J.R.R. Tolkien's idea that the elements of a good fairy tale are "fantasy, recovery, escape, and consolation—recovery from deep despair, escape from some great danger, but, most of all, consolation" (143). The consolation comes in the form of a happy ending. Bettelheim himself would add the element of threat to physical or moral existence to Tolkien's list, as the child experiences their life as filled with dangers and unpredictable turns, such as when a normally loving parent becomes terrifying. Many fairy tales feature young protagonists being cast out on their own, which speaks to the terror of separation anxiety, the greatest threat of all as it hinders our survival and belonging. In saccharine modern fairy tales, the threats are minimized, meaning that the child often feels that the sense of justice has not prevailed.

On the Telling of Fairy Stories

Bettelheim insists that fairy tales work better when they are told to a child by an adult who has an active investment in both the child and the tale. Indeed, fairy tales evolved over the generations with each narrator adapting the story according to their unconscious instinct of what the child needed from the story. Often, children themselves will intervene, adding and embellishing details that speak to them, and the fantastical nature of the tales makes space for such spontaneous adaptations.

Rather than attempting to teach a moral through the telling of fairy tales, parents should focus on the "shared experience of enjoying the tale" (154), as child and parent become aware of which components speak to each other. The adult's investment in the emotional aspects of the fairy tale creates in the child listener a sense of empathy that in turn makes them feel secure and more optimistic about growing up. The fairy tale will work on the child's mind over time, as some elements will provoke immediate responsiveness, while the other will take deeper root in the unconscious.

Part 1 Analysis

In the first half of his text, Bettelheim argues fairy tales' essential role in externalizing the chaotic internal process of the pre-oedipal and oedipal child. For example, the bottled-up jinny in the "Fisherman and the Jinny" gives words and images to a child's incomprehensible fury after being abandoned, while stories like "The Three Feathers" relate the universal childhood experience of feeling small and ignorant in a world of older, more sophisticated people. The youngest child's triumph in "The Three Feathers," in addition to seeing how, collectively, the three little pigs can evolve their knowledge to escape the wolf, gives the child hope that they, too, can develop the tools to succeed. Here, Bettelheim emphasizes that though fairy tale protagonists may be casually given the attribute of prince or princess, they are everyday figures with whom the child can identify, unlike the nobles of myths. The security that comes in the form of a happy ending—which reassures that even after the most frightening obstacles, everything will be okay—creates resilience and hope. Crucially, instead of being sheltered from challenge, it is being able to identify with the protagonist and see them victorious that gives the child confidence.

Bettelheim emphasizes that the fantastical worlds of fairy tales provide a scope onto which the child to project their anxieties; one that they would have never been able to invent by themselves through play. Guided by the tale, the child can then improvise on the situation, living vicariously through the faraway protagonists in helpfully vague geographical settings. For example, the distance of a European forest creates some safety between the city-dwelling child and the tale's fearsome supernatural events, and the child now has a container for the narrative that parallels their most fraught psychic experiences. Bettelheim argues that the child requires an active engagement with the fairy tale to receive its benefits and thus warns that illustrated stories prevent children from creating vivid worlds that are personal to them. Through repeated telling by an emotionally invested parent, the tale makes its way into the child's unconscious and meets them at their particular stage of development.

From a psychoanalytic perspective, a key component of fairy tales is how they encourage a child's personality integration. Through the fantastical scenarios that harmonize with a child's animist view of the world, the fairy tale enables a child to see all aspects of their personality reflected. Most of all, they gain the reassurance that the *id*, the instinctual facet of the personality that dominates and overwhelms the young child, can be brought under control and even put to good service by a well-developed ego and superego. Bettelheim views the fairy tale as uniquely capable in aiding personality integration, as realistic narratives do not sufficiently portray the animality of the subconscious and do nothing to reassure the child that they are not alone with their violent fantasies. In contrast, the fairy tale reminds them that even admirable heroes struggle with feelings like their own.

As the reader progresses through Bettelheim's studies of personality integration, they may notice that women and girls play a disproportionate role in bringing an animalistic, id-dominated male into superego and ego submission. While this, in a way, empowers women and presents them as more controlled and superior, it also feeds into the predominant cultural stereotypes that women have few sexual desires of their own and are responsible for containing men's rampant sexuality. The fairy tales that Bettelheim presents show that the heroines are always successful in this endeavor and so offer little consolation to victims of abuse or rape. Moreover, while Bettelheim regards that the fairy tale's depiction of women as supremely giving and self-sacrificing is positive, modern female readers may think this view is limited and incorrect.

Part 2

Part 2 Summary: "In Fairy Land"

"Hansel and Gretel"

The Brothers Grimm story of Hansel and Gretel begins with a brother and sister being sent away by their poor parents, who can no longer feed them. Bettelheim writes how this corresponds to a child's anxiety of being abandoned and left to starve by their caregivers. Hansel and Gretel become fixated on food, and Hansel's starvation anxiety leads him to make the foolish choice of leaving a trail of breadcrumbs back to the home. The initial intention to return home, in Bettelheim's view, symbolizes the child's attempt to return to dependency after being thrust into independence. An intervening bird who eats the bread crumb trail symbolizes the outside world forcing the children out of such regression.

The story's famous gingerbread house, which Hansel and Gretel encounter in the woods and immediately begin eating, symbolizes the return to an oral stage of development (a developmental stage in Freudian psychology), where the children could rely on an all-giving mother's body to nourish them. Bettelheim explains that "it is the original all-giving mother, whom every child hopes to find again later somewhere out in the world, when his own mother begins to make demands and impose restrictions" (161). The gingerbread house owner, who initially feeds the children more, seems like a stand-in for the good mother—however, she is a wicked witch who wants to eat the children. Her plans "finally force the children to recognize the dangers of unrestrained oral greed and dependence" (162). This is because the witch speaks to the children's anxiety that the original good mother was not feeding them for their own benefit, but rather to eat them.

The children learn to submit their id-dominated appetites to the mastery of the ego as they come up with a plan to trick the witch and shove her into the oven. When they take the witch's jewels back home, they have a new mature role as contributors to the parental home, rather than being its mere passive recipients.

Facing the exaggerated danger of the witch indicates Hansel and Gretel's newfound ability to cope with the world's dangers, and the story provides a hopeful model for the child.

"Little Red Riding Hood"

As with "Hansel and Gretel," the predominant theme of "Little Red Riding Hood" is being devoured. However, Little Red Riding Hood—or Little Red Cap, as she is in the Brothers Grimm version—is a pubertal child who encounters temptations in line with her stage of development. Rather than being intimidated by the outside world, Little Red Riding Hood is enchanted by its beauty and suggestible to the wolf's idea that she should enjoy the pretty road to her grandmother's house rather than doing her duty and going straight there to deliver the food. Here, Bettelheim interprets the plot to mean that Little Red Riding Hood is regressing from the reality principle to the pleasure principle as her curiosity tempts her to discover the world outside of the home. Bettelheim emphasizes that the wolf would have no devouring power unless part of him appealed to Little Red Riding Hood's own asocial, id-based tendencies. For Bettelheim, this is because as she enters puberty, Little Red Riding Hood returns to the oedipal stage of wanting to seduce her father away from her mother. The father is unmentioned by the narrative; however, Bettelheim suspects that he is "in hidden form" in the complementary forms of hunter and wolf, whereby the wolf represents the danger of overwhelming oedipal feelings, while the hunter represents the rescuer (178). Thus, the wolf is the seductive, dangerous half of this father figure, while the rescuing woodcutter is his protective counterpart. According to Bettelheim, the story teaches young girls that they should not seek to outdo their mothers in seduction of the father or a figure like him, but should instead be content to be protected by him a while longer, until they are truly sexually mature.

Bettelheim observes that Little Red Riding Hood points the way to her grandmother's house, thus unconsciously giving the wolf permission to devour her grandmother. In Bettelheim's view, this is a result of Little Red Riding Hood's "budding sexuality, for which she is not yet emotionally mature enough" (173). The author asserts that the seductive red cap or red hood given to the girl by her mother is too mature for a girl of her age and invites attention for which she is not ready. Thus, Little Red Riding Hood directs the wolf to her grandmother's house in the hope that this more mature, sexually prepared woman can satisfy his appetites. However, seeking to avoid the danger of encountering the wolf alone nearly leads to Little Red Riding Hood's ruin. From the wolf's perspective, getting rid of the grandmother first, rather than devouring Little Red Riding Hood on the spot, indicates that as soon as a mother figure is done away with, the path will be cleared for acting on his desires.

The wolf's devouring of Little Red Riding Hood and her grandmother should be taken symbolically rather than literally. Children, better than adults, can understand that Little Red Riding Hood dies when she is eaten by the wolf and is reborn when the hunter cuts open his belly. Her death symbolizes the end of her premature attempts to cope with the world, while her rebirth indicates her ascendance to a more mature plane of existence where she is ready to meet the world and its challenges.

"Jack and the Beanstalk"

There are many variations of "Jack and the Beanstalk," and Bettelheim believes all deal with the different phases of a boy's sexual development. A lesser-known English version called "Jack and His Bargains" tells of a rebellious son who sells his father's cow at a fair for a magic stick which will defeat all enemies. Jack uses this stick to defeat his father and goes again to the fair where the man gives him a fiddle and a bee that plays beautiful songs. He uses the latter two gifts to win the heart of an unsmiling princess. However, Jack refrains from making a move on her in bed for the first three nights, and her angry father throws him into a pit of wild animals. When Jack uses his magic stick to tame the beasts, the princess marvels at "what a proper man he was" (185), and they properly marry and have many children. For Bettelheim, the stick has obvious phallic associations as it represents the phallic stage of development where the child believes that its own body has magical powers. Entering this stage enables Jack to defeat his father and the princess' other suitors; however, when he delays consummating the marriage, it indicates that he subjugates the tendencies of his id, represented by the wild animals he defeats, with an ego-managed self-control. He thereby truly comes of age.

While "Jack and the Beanstalk" deals with a younger boy, it similarly tackles the theme of masculine development, according to Bettelheim. The story begins with the end of a beloved cow's milk-giving days, signaling the completion of Jack's oral stage of development. In contrast, Jack's accession to the magic beans indicates a progression to the phallic stage, where he finds security in a "fantastically exaggerated belief in what his body and its organs will do for him" (189). Here, this is a stage of sexual development where the boy thinks he can rely all on his own body for fulfillment. As the seeds are scattered to grow a vertiginous beanstalk, Jack believes he will achieve ascendence by climbing to the top, relying on the strength of his young body. At the top of the beanstalk, an ogre figure, representative of a father, presents Jack with his oedipal conflict when Jack wishes to replace the father-figure ogre.

Jack matures where he realizes that he cannot rely forever on the magic solutions suggested to him by the phallic stage. He therefore cuts down the beanstalk and, as a result, relinquishes the idea that the father is a destructive ogre. Instead, Jack will try to live in the real world during his next phase of development.

The Jealous Queen in "Snow White" and the Myth of Oedipus

Fairy tales encourage not only the child to resolve their oedipal struggles, but the parent as well. Figures like the jealous queen in "Snow White" show how a parent can become consumed by the envy they feel towards their child and the fear that the latter will surpass them. This parallels King Laius' fear of his son Oedipus as a competitor and his wish to destroy him. The fairy tale does not explain the motivation behind the parent's jealousy; however, Bettelheim imagines a past wound obstructs the queen's love for her child.

For Bettelheim, it is a reassuring idea that the parent may be as jealous of the child as the child is of a parent. He argues that reading fairy tales on this subject may be constructive in dealing with such issues of envy. However, more importantly, "the fairy tale reassures the child that he need not be afraid of parental jealousy where it may exist, because he will survive successfully, whatever complications these feelings may create temporarily" (195). While oedipal myths end tragically, fairy tale protagonists who have resolved oedipal conflicts give the child hope on the journey to become themselves.

"Snow White"

Some versions of "Snow White" make the oedipal competition between mother and daughter explicit, as they feature a father figure wishing for a girl as white as snow, with cheeks as red as blood, and hair as black as a raven's feathers. When such a girl is born, this arouses jealousy in the mother, who finds ways to get rid of the girl. In the Brothers Grimm version, it is the mother who wishes for a daughter with Snow White's coloring; after the mother dies, the stepmother who replaces her is the one who wishes to destroy Snow White.

Bettelheim views the stepmother as a narcissistic figure who is threatened by her stepdaughter's independent existence and the idea that she may one day have a beauty that will eclipse her own. Snow White thus becomes competition, in the stepmother's eyes, for the father's affections. Bettelheim stipulates that at a preconscious level, Snow White may be jealous of the attention her father pays his wife, as she may wish that energy was bestowed upon herself. However, Snow White's narcissism causes her to project her jealous feelings onto the queen, who she believes wants to destroy her. Thus, the "pubertal girl's oedipal struggle" is "acted around the mother as competitor" (205). Bettelheim conjectures that the queen's famous magic mirror speaks in Snow White's voice. As a little girl, Snow White thinks her mother the most beautiful person who ever lived—but, as she grows, her adolescent fancy leads her to believe that she herself is the fairest one. Still, says Bettelheim, the adolescent's wish to surpass the same-sex parent is also a fear, because they dread the idea that the still more powerful parent will find out and punish them.

When Snow White evades the stepmother's attempts to eat her, she lives for a while in the woods with seven hard-working dwarves. For Bettelheim, this is a period when the pubescent girl attempts to re-enter her latency phase and so escape the perils of adolescence. He regards the dwarves as half-child, half-adult beings who are stuck in the phallic stage of development and thus, never ascending to the genital stage, do not understand Snow White's desires. These desires come to the fore when Snow White is tempted by the disguised stepmother's gifts, which are figure-enhancing items that appeal to the girl's vanity. These gifts include a poison comb and a corset that the stepmother laces so tight that Snow White falls down in a deathlike faint. Each time, the dwarves come to Snow White's rescue, and she reenters her latency phase. Bettelheim regards that the comb, for example, is "'poisonous' to Snow White in her early, immature adolescent state" as she is tempted to be a sexual being but not yet able to deal with its consequences (212). The final temptation is the apple, of which the Queen eats the white half, giving Snow White the red poisonous half. Red symbolizes eroticism and the death of Snow White's pre-sexual being. The sleep that follows is like a final gestation period in which she revives enough for maturity and the prince who rescues her. Such rest is necessary to the assumption of a higher consciousness.

"Goldilocks and the Three Bears"

Like "Snow White," "Goldilocks" tells the story of a little girl lost in the woods and finding a house that has been temporarily abandoned by its inhabitants. However, unlike with "Snow White," the reader is not told why Goldilocks is in this predicament; she seems to come "from nowhere and has no place to go" (218).

Arriving at the three bears' house, Goldilocks lands upon the complete family setup. Although the bears are away from home, the customized furniture implies that father, mother, and baby bear know their roles. In contrast, Goldilocks is an imposter who struggles to find an identity. Goldilocks tries each bears' porridge, chair, and bed as an experiment for where she fits in. Bettelheim argues that the number three is essential to "Goldilocks," symbolizing the search for a personal and social identity as the child "must learn with whom he ought to identify as he grows up, and who is suitable to become his life's companion, and with it also his sexual partner" (220). Bettelheim posits that Goldilocks's sampling of father bear's dish, chair, and bed first indicates her expression of a typical girl's oedipal wish to be close to her father. When she finds the father's things do not suit her, she tries on the mother's for size. The mother bear's food and furniture symbolize the oral stage of development, when Goldilocks was denied nothing—however, they are unsuitable for Goldilocks at this more advanced stage. The baby bear's food and furniture seem perfectly adequate; however, Goldilocks is too heavy for the chair, and it breaks. This indicates that she does not exactly fit in with the child figure in the family, either. Goldilocks thus remains an imposter, and there is no happy ending for her.

Given the Goldilocks story's ambiguity, a child's experience of the tale will depend very much on how the parent narrates it and how sympathetic they are with a child's wish to see how adults live and explore their secrets.

"The Sleeping Beauty"

Bettelheim characterizes adolescence as a stage where intervals of lethargy alternate with frenetic activity. "The Sleeping Beauty" emphasizes that a period of quiet concentration and self-focus reflects the time around the first menstruation, when girls become self-involved and sleepy. Boys also may become more introverted during puberty. The fairy tale's message is that "after having gathered strength in solitude they now have to become themselves" (226), as a deep sleep is a prelude to maturation.

The motif of delay is apparent in "The Sleeping Beauty" from the time of the heroine's conception. Her parents struggle to conceive her for years and almost give up hope when, in the Grimms' version, a frog accompanies her mother into the bath and tells her that her wishes will be fulfilled. Then, at the child's christening, the 13th evil fairy's curse that she will prick her finger on a spindle and die—the number 13 being a parallel to the number of menstrual cycles a woman typically has in a year—gets modified into the idea that she will sleep for a hundred years. Fifteen, the projected age for spindle-pricking, was also the typical age of first menstruation for girls in previous centuries. While the king orders all the spindles to be burnt to prevent the girl's encounter with a spindle, the girl's ability to find one shows that "whatever precautions a father takes, when the daughter is ripe for it, puberty will set in" (232). The girl, who is overwhelmed by the sight of bleeding, falls into a sleep that withdraws her from the world and protects her from immature sexual encounters.

The thorns that grow around her castle indicate her unreadiness for sexuality while the somnolent state of everything around her, indicates her insensitivity to the world. When the time is ripe however, the thorns turn into flowers as the girl's natural development solves her pubertal woes. The princess' sleep can be seen as a kind of narcissistic withdrawal, which can only be broken by the prince and his kiss, which directs her eroticism outwards.

Children will interpret "The Sleeping Beauty" differently according to their stage of development. While a young child will view her reawakening as her becoming herself, for an older child it will symbolize the move towards a harmonious coexistence with another after a period of self-focus.

"Cinderella"

"Cinderella," a story with many variations that likely originated in China in the ninth century A.D., is the archetypal fairy tale about sibling rivalry. Children of both sexes identify with Cinderella's feeling less capable and valuable than her siblings, even if they can rationally conceive that their predicament is not as harsh as Cinderella's. The tale enables the child to own their inherent worthiness, while the happy ending gives them hope that they will surpass their siblings.

Bettelheim stipulates that the root of sibling rivalry is the child's feelings not about their siblings but towards their parents. When the period of the parents' making demands on the child succeeds the oral stage, where all their needs are met, the child begins to see their siblings as rivals, "fearing that in comparison to them he cannot win his parents' love and esteem" (238). As a way of unconsciously dealing with their inferiority, even only children can contemplate fictitious siblings whom their parents would prefer to them.

Bettelheim argues that Cinderella's obscure creeping about the ashes at the beginning of the tale is significant, as young children secretly relate to this state of degradation. They realize that their secret habits and wishes, including an oedipal desire to get rid of the same-sex parent, would be shameful were they to come to light. Thus, seeing Cinderella dirty amongst the ashes is of comfort to these children, because Cinderella is ultimately innocent and good, and they hope that they will be perceived in an analogous way. The character also allows children to harbor their feelings of superiority to their siblings. Such feelings of personal superiority are a relic from the phase of primary narcissism prior to the oedipal phase—a time when a child feels at the center of the parents' world, and so there is no reason for jealousy. Cinderella, too, enjoyed this period of primary narcissism as, prior to her father's union with her stepmother, there was a benign real mother who denied her nothing and established a basic trust in herself and the world. Bettelheim regards Cinderella's obsession with the hearth and ashes as an attempt to hold onto the original nurturing mother, who, like the hearth, was at the center of warmth and nourishment. However, this is futile because the mother figure in Cinderella's life is no longer the all-providing mother of infancy but the denying stepmother, who sets her tasks such as separating lentils from a pile of ashes in under two hours. The basic trust established by the original mother enables Cinderella to perform such a task.

For Bettelheim, Cinderella's character journey is one of ceasing to live in the past and through hard work, attaining the stage in development where she is ready for marriage. Cinderella's ambivalence about growing up is evident in her three trips to the ball. Bettelheim argues that, as with other fairy tales, the number three signifies the child's position in the family in relation to their parents, while Cinderella's flight from the prince and leaving her glass slipper indicates an anxiety about retaining her virginity. However, Bettelheim also argues that it is important to Cinderella that her would-be-lover sees her not in her splendid disguise, but in her degraded state amongst the ashes. Then, he can fall in love with the essence of her and not just an appearance.

The material of the slipper at the center of Cinderella, which enables the prince to identify her as the rightful bride, varies according to the tale's teller. The famous glass slipper comes from the version by the French pioneer of courtly fairy tales, Charles Perrault. Bettelheim reads further psychoanalytic symbolism into the shoe: On the one hand, it symbolizes the vagina as a place "into which some part of the body can slip and fit tightly" (265), while the idea that it cannot be stretched is resonant of the hymen, which breaks upon first intercourse. The prince's wish for a bride who fits the shoe indicates his desire for a specific type of femininity. According to the patriarchal expectation that women should be smaller and daintier than men, the fact that Cinderella's feet are smaller than her sisters' indicates that she is more feminine. The sisters mutilate their feet in order to pass as the rightful bride, however, each time, chanting birds give them away, drawing the prince's attention to the blood. For Bettelheim, the sisters engage in "self-castration to prove their femininity" (268). However, in doing so, the bleeding also symbolizes menstrual blood, which (again, in a patriarchal society) indicates that they are less virginal than Cinderella, who does not bleed when her feet enter the slipper. Bettelheim argues that Cinderella's lack of bleeding eases the prince's unconscious fear of menstruation. This indicates further that her sexuality is not predatory like her sisters' but rather patient and yielding. In addition to Cinderella's integrity, her willingness to be seen as her dirty self is what makes her the true bride. However, despite Cinderella's continence, her willingness to be seen amongst the ashes (in addition to her initiative in shoeing her own foot) indicates her desire for a sexual union with the prince.

Overall, says Bettelheim, the story of Cinderella reassures parents that they may have to take up the position of "stepparents" (withholding, unindulgent figures) in their children's own interest. Next, it reassures children of the necessity of undergoing a servile, Cinderella-like existence for a time in which they find and can prove their worth.

The Animal-Groom Cycle of Fairy Tales

I: "The Struggle for Maturity"

Bettelheim argues that the fairy tales that he has discussed thus far offer little information about what being in love means. Instead, stories such as "Snow White" and "Cinderella" focus on the self-development needed to reach a level of maturity where one can fall in love. However, this is not enough as "one becomes a complete human being who has achieved all his potentialities only if, in addition to being oneself, one is at the same time able and happy to be oneself with another" (279). One must also reverse earlier attitudes, which repressed and shamed sexual impulses, with the idea that sexuality can be redeemed through love and experienced as beautiful and natural. The fairy tale heroines' lack of carnal feelings towards their rescuing princes, claims Bettelheim, "is actually the void left by their repression, and this repression must be undone" before a happy marriage, complete with a healthy sex life, can be achieved (280).

Bettelheim believes that fairy tales are a great way for children to learn about sex, as children can respond to the symbolic language and imagery in their stories according to their stage in development.

II: "The Fairy Tale of One Who Went Forth to Learn Fear"

The author contends that this idea—of ridding oneself of sexual repression before achieving happiness in marriage—is expressed most cogently in a Brothers Grimm story about a hero who feels that he must learn to shudder upon entering the institution. After many attempts to feel fear, the hero finally learns to shudder when his new wife pours a pail of freezing water and little fish over him in their marriage bed. Bettelheim argues that the hero lost his ability to shudder or feel fear so "that he would not have to face the feelings which overcome him in the marital bed—that is, sexual emotions. But without these feelings [...] he is not a full person" (281). By making the hero shudder, the wife not only makes him vulnerable but restores his humanity. He is only fit to be united with another when a full spectrum of feelings are available to him.

III: "The Animal Groom"

Bettelheim next addresses stories featuring an animal groom, whereby a beast is transfigured into a magnificent human through the love of a woman. The author believes that such stories illustrate that, for love to be present, "a radical change in previously held attitudes about sex is absolutely necessary" (282). In the animal groom fairy tales, a man is changed into a beast by a sorceress, for reasons that remain ambiguous. For Bettelheim, this sorceress is a mother-figure who passes on the taboo that sex is animal-like and therefore demeaning. It is only a worthy heroine's devotion that can disenchant the hero from his state of apparent animality. She can do this if she is willing to "transfer—and transform—this oedipal love for her father most freely and happily to her lover" (284). Thus, the girl's oedipal complex is resolved, while previously taboo sexuality is redeemed.

IV: "Snow-White and Rose Red"

In the Grimms' "Snow White and Rose-Red," the heroines must rescue a dwarf who changed a human into a bear three times. In doing so, the girls must "exorcise" the bear's "nasty nature in the form of a dwarf for an animal-like relation to become a human one" (286). Here, Bettelheim's analysis reflects how a chauvinistic culture projected sexual perversion onto the non-standard anatomy of the dwarf. However, the story's moral is that the heroine needs to change her attitude to sex, "because as long as sex appears to her as ugly and animal-like it remains animalistic in the male" (286). Both partners need to be able to enjoy sex for it to become a human interaction.

V: "The Frog King"

"The Frog King" tells the story of a little princess whose precious golden ball falls into a well. A frog rescues the ball and asks that, in return, he should sit beside her, drink from her glass, and accompany her to bed. The princess agrees but does not intend to heed the frog's request. However, the frog tracks her down, and her father, the king, insists that she keep her promise to the frog.

For Bettelheim, the princess' golden ball represents "an as yet undeveloped narcissistic psyche: it contains all potentials, none yet realized" (287). However, when it falls into the well, disenchantment that signals the end of childhood ensues and only the frog can restore her state of perfection. The frog, with its slimy amphibian nature, represents childish anxieties about sexuality. It's phallic form and behavior may at first seem disgusting to a green child, but it is also an agent of restoring their happiness in a more mature form. The king aligns with the superego to ensure that the princess keeps her promise to the frog.

While the princess begins the narrative unfeeling and self-centered, as the frog gets closer to her, she begins to feel many emotions. Indeed, her first feeling is rage, when she throws the frog against the wall. This act changes the frog into the prince, as "the stronger her feelings become, she becomes more a person" (288). As she becomes herself, the frog resumes his original form as a prince. The transformation reveals sexuality's true beauty.

The frog itself also undergoes sexual maturation, as he begins with the infantile wish for symbiosis with the princess, represented by eating from her place and drinking from her cup. Her act of throwing him against the wall propels him out of this state and thus liberates him from his immature existence. The frog symbolizes psychosexual development because it is an animal that undergoes a radical transformation during its lifetime.

Bettelheim suggests that this fairy tale is a comfort to children learning about sex as it acknowledges and respects their initial disgust. As a result, the child trusts the tale and its message that their original repulsion will turn into something beautiful.

"Cupid and Psyche"

The earliest of the beast bridegroom stories is the classical myth Cupid and Psyche, written by Apuleius in the second century A.D. The goddess Aphrodite enviously punishes Psyche, the youngest and most beautiful daughter of three, by asking her son Eros (Cupid is the Latin version of the name, and Bettelheim uses both interchangeably) to make Psyche fall in love with the most "grotesque" of men. Eros disobeys his mother and presents himself as Psyche's husband. When Psyche complains of loneliness, Eros invites over her sisters to keep her company. As they are jealous of her beauty, they tell Psyche that "what she cohabits and is pregnant by is 'a huge serpent with a thousand coils'" (292). They persuade Psyche to sever this gross phallic appendage at night, while Eros is sleeping. However, when light falls onto Eros, Psyche realizes his beauty and refrains from the act of castration. Although Psyche regrets her actions, she must undergo serious tribulations, including entry into the underworld before she can be reunited with Eros.

For Bettelheim, Psyche's anxiety of the snake "gives visual expression to the inexperienced girl's formless sexual anxieties" (293). Whilst Psyche loves Eros, she is upset at his severance of her maidenhood and seeks to punish him by attacking his virility—hence her castrating him. However, Eros is never actually a beast, but Psyche's prejudices mistake him for one.

"The Enchanted Pig"

In a little-known Romanian fairy tale "The Enchanted Pig," a youngest daughter is married off to a creature who is a man by night but a pig by day. While the girl follows a witch's recommendation to tie her husband's leg at night in order to stop him turning into a pig by day, this does not work. Her husband now leaves, telling her they shall not meet until she undergoes severe tribulations. These tribulations are "endless wanderings" that result in her having to give up her little finger in order to use it as the final rung of a ladder that helps her reach her husband and return him to a fully human state (296).

In this story, too, says Bettelheim, the animal husband is a figment of the girl's sexual anxieties and the learned cultural assumption that females should experience sex as animalistic. In Bettelheim's view, the same woman may enjoy sex with her husband at night, but resent him for his defilement of her virginity by day. The wanderings and tribulations endured by the female protagonists of this story indicate that to divest one's sexual anxieties, "one must grow as a person, and unfortunately much of this growth can be achieved only through suffering" (298). In contrast to the cultural expectations of female passivity in sex, the female must make as much of an effort as the male to achieve satisfaction in this area.

"Bluebeard"

The many variations of the "Bluebeard" tale feature the common motif of a wife being forbidden to enter a room in a husband's absence, and the husband's murderous rage when he discovers she has done so. In the room are the mutilated bodies of all the other disobedient, unfaithful wives. Bettelheim speculates that the gruesome sight in the room may be a "creation of her own anxious fantasies; or that she has betrayed her husband, but hopes he won't find out" (301). In the Grimm Brothers' version, "Fitcher's Bird," the wife is given an egg to hold with her, and the egg becomes bloodied, symbolizing her transgression as she enters. Bettelheim theorizes that even the child understands from the motif of the bloodied egg that the wife has committed a sexual indiscretion. For children, Bluebeard's room symbolizes the fascination and fear of adult sexuality, in addition to the hypothesis that it is full of secrets. In Bettelheim's analysis, "Bluebeard" is a cautionary tale that warns women against excessive sexual curiosity and men against excessive sexual jealousy, which can make them as beastly as Bluebeard.

"Beauty and the Beast"

Bettelheim draws his study of "Beauty and the Beast" from the 1757 version by Madame Leprince de Beaumont. For Bettelheim, this tale illustrates the healthy transference of a girl's oedipal love for her father to her future husband. Beauty's encounter with the Beast begins when her father gets lost in the act of seeking the rose that Beauty desires. The Beast seizes Beauty's father and says that he will only release him if one of the daughters can come in his place. Beauty agrees to go to the Beast's palace in her father's place. At first, Beauty is the Beast's platonic guest and lives a life of ease at the palace, only greeting him at dinner. At one stage, she begins to look forward to his visits, if only to break her loneliness. However, she refuses the Beast's marriage proposal. According to Bettelheim, the broken rose symbolizes the loss of virginity and "may seem to both father and daughter as if she would have to suffer some 'beastly' experience" (306). At the castle, Beauty's desire to delay marriage evokes her anxieties about sexuality and her preference of an asexual relationship and an independent lifestyle that has the quality of a "narcissistic non-existence" (307).

Beauty returns to a state of feeling and reciprocity when she discovers, with the aid of a magic mirror, that her father is sick and needs her. The Beast allows her to escape for a week, however, he warns her that he himself will die if she delays her return. In her absence, the Beast pines away, and Beauty realizes her love for him and her desire to be his wife. She thus transfers her oedipal longing for her father onto the Beast. Their love also symbolizes the healing of the rift between the spiritual and animal aspects of humanity. Without Beauty's love, the animal beast will perish. When she reciprocates, turning his passion into human devotion, he is transformed back into a prince. In psychoanalytic terms, their connection represents the superego's socialization of the id.

Bettelheim ends his work by emphasizing that the fairy tale functions as a magic mirror that reflects the self and shows the steps required to progress from immaturity to the next stage of human development.

Part 2 Analysis

The second part of Bettelheim's book shows the manifold applications that the most popular fairy tales can have on a child's psyche at different stages of development. While he demonstrates that children adapt the narrative and imagery of the tales to suit their current psychic experiences, he focuses especially on puberty.

With the Animal Groom cycle of tales, Bettelheim argues that fairy tales are useful in sex education because they acknowledge and even empathize with a child's disgust and fascination with sex. The symbol of the frog in "The Frog King" illustrates a child's ambivalent response to sexual realities, while tales such as "Beauty and the Beast" illustrate how sexuality can make a life richer and more connected than the narcissism of the preceding phallic and latent stages or the immature oedipal loyalty to the opposite-sex parent. These stories, says Bettelheim, also encourage the cultivation of depth, as children identify with heroines who look beyond the frightening appearance of beasts to appreciate the essence of their being. This prepares a child for changing their mind about sexuality and for the fact that this might require time and challenging life experiences.

Still, Bettelheim presents disgust with sexuality as a particularly female trait, either engendered by jealous older women or as an intrinsic reluctance to lose one's virginity. While Bettelheim reflects the liberal attitudes of the 1970s, stipulating that sexuality is healthy for women, he does not take much interest in the cultural attitudes that have made it a taboo. This lessens the depth and effectiveness of his argument.

In this section, too, Bettelheim shows how some of the tales are tailored specifically to boys or girls to demonstrate how sojourns in the thorny realm of puberty culminate in an adult self that can participate in the social realm. For example, in his analysis of *Jack and the Beanstalk*, Bettelheim shows the progression of different stages of development and the necessity for not stagnating in any phase. While the magic seeds and the tall stalk represent the phallic stage in development (when Jack replaces reliance on his mother with autonomy and a belief in his body's capability), the magic of this period, which is akin to masturbation, must give way to seeking a relationship with the world. Here, the fairy tale guides the child to see that they must give up a seemingly magical phase of their existence when it is no longer helpful to their development. It thus leads them through fairy land only to better plant their feet in the real world.

With regard to pubertal girls, Bettelheim addresses the specific challenge of menstruation, the rite of passage that, traditionally, marks the transition from girlhood to womanhood. Bettelheim continually emphasizes that in centuries prior to the 20th, menarche typically happened at 15, which is later than today. Thus, menstruation was often the precursor to sexuality and marriage. While Bettelheim's observation that menstruation can be a shocking event for girls may be true, his explanation of it in "The Sleeping Beauty" and "Cinderella" reflects male and not female anxiety around this former taboo. For example, in "The Sleeping Beauty" where the prick of a finger on a spindle signifies a first period, it is the king who wishes "to prevent his daughter from experiencing the fatal bleeding" (232). Similarly, in "Cinderella," the sisters' mutilated, bleeding feet signal menstruation whilst Cinderella's small, untarnished foot indicates a pre-menstrual virginal stage. Bettelheim's judgment that "the girl who permits her bleeding to be seen, particularly by a man—as the stepsisters with their bleeding feet cannot help doing—is not only coarse, but certainly less virginal than the one who does not bleed," is a projection of patriarchal disgust at a natural female bodily process (268). Such an attitude, far from being helpful, may cause a pubescent girl to feel shame about her body, even as Bettelheim (ironically) claims that Cinderella's charm is her willingness to be seen by the prince as she truly is, in the abjection of ashes. Bettelheim's contradictory message about how comfortable a girl should be with her body and true self reflects patriarchal society's desire to compare women and pit them against each other in order to diminish their power.

Similarly, while Bettelheim's discussion of Snow White's rivalry with her stepmother reflects the internal oedipal conflicts between a young girl and her mother, he overlooks the influence that patriarchal culture has in forcefully engendering this vanity. Bettelheim takes it as given that the young, blossoming daughter should overtake the aging mother in influence, without questioning the external cultural belief system that deems that this should be the case. He cannot foresee a happy ending where Snow White and her mother live in harmony, nor does he think it would be an advantage for fairy tales to encourage the child to imagine such an event.

Key Figures

Bruno Bettelheim

The author, Bruno Bettelheim (1903-1990) was born in Vienna, Austria, where he worked in his family's lumber business until 1938, when the Nazis invaded Austria and placed him in a concentration camp at Dachau, Germany because he was Jewish. On being released in 1939, he moved to the United States. He embarked on his interest in psychology when he became a research associate with the Progressive Education Association at the University of Chicago. By 1944, he had become an associate professor of psychology there, as well as the head of the Sonia Shankman Orthogenic School, where he worked with children with autism. He was interested in applying psychoanalytic principles to the troubles the children faced, and he published on the topic in books titled *Love is Not Enough* (1950) and *Truants from Life* (1954). Bettelheim became a public intellectual, even appearing on the Dick Cavett show in 1979; however, there was a shadow side to his personality. Other scholars, including Jack Zipes, claimed that Bettelheim fabricated his credentials and that much of his work, including that for *The Uses of Enchantment* (1976), was plagiarized. There were also rumors that he physically abused some of the children under his care at the Sonia Shankman school. He lived with depression, and, following the death of his wife in 1984 and a stroke in 1987, he died by suicide.

Bettelheim wrote *The Uses of Enchantment* during his retirement. It has few autobiographical details, although it is peppered with case studies of the children he encountered during his work. He illustrates how fairy tale motifs have helped children figure out their problems; for example, how a girl who was jealous of her sister "was very fond of 'Cinderella,' since the story offered her material with which to act out her feelings, and because without the story's imagery she would have been hard pressed to comprehend and express them" (241). Such instances indicate that Bettelheim's findings derive from close observation of small children and their interaction with fairy tales over time.

Bettelheim's focus on European fairy tales and his preference for the Grimm Brothers is a symptom of his Germanic background. Bettelheim says that he, like the famous German poet Goethe, was told these tales by his mother, and the local variants of the stories they espoused were likely to be modifications of the Grimm Brothers' tales. Thus, his preference of the Grimm Brothers' work does not have a meritocratic basis but is the result of his heritage and early experience. As Bettelheim was exiled from his country, time and distance may have made him see it as the land of fairy tales. From an experiential point of view, the extreme violence the Nazis perpetrated on Jews like him was akin to fairy tale heroes' mistreatment at the hands of stepmothers and ogres. Moving to America would have offered a safe distance from the old country; whilst at the same time, he understood that the difficulties faced in Europe were also present in life in the States.

Sigmund Freud

Sigmund Freud (1856-1939) came from an Austrian Jewish background and is known as the father of psychoanalysis. Psychoanalysis is a therapeutic system derived from the notion that human thought and behavior are the result of unconscious phenomena as well as conscious ones. Thus, the patient may be suffering from things that are beyond their conscious control, including repressed memories and preoccupations. Freud's work became highly influential during the 20th century, and psychoanalysts in both Europe and America modeled their practices on his teachings. Bettelheim was one of these disciples, and he regularly cites Freud in *The Uses of Enchantment*.

Freud himself was no stranger to using literature and myth to illustrate psychoanalytic motifs. In "The Theme of the Three Caskets" (1913) he references folk tales where protagonists must choose between three competing elements. However, the most famous use of myth in Freud's oeuvre is that of Oedipus who kills his father and marries his mother (however, unlike Freud's narrative for the Oedipus complex, the ancient Greek Oedipus does these things unwittingly). Bettelheim makes ample use of Freud's ideas as he examines portrayals of the Oedipus complex in fairy tales and how this, in turn, influences child readers. Bettelheim also draws upon Freud's division of the personality into the component parts of id, superego and ego, showing how fairy tales, unlike the contemporary children's literature, give free rein to an id that matches children's most violent fantasies.

Carl Jung

Carl Jung (1875-1961) was a Swiss psychologist and psychiatrist whose work was, in many ways, a response to Freud's psychoanalysis. He coined the idea of the two most popular personality types—introvert and extrovert—and studied myths and folktales extensively to develop theories of archetypes and the collective unconscious. Whereas Freud focused on an individual's inner repressed experiences, Jung was interested in the unconscious motifs of humanity as a whole.

Bettelheim is less overtly influenced by Jung than by Freud; however, his discussion of fairy tale motifs as universally applicable has much in common with Jung's idea of a collective unconscious. He cites how Jungian psychologists view fairy tales and myths as being full of symbols that "suggest the need for gaining a higher state of selfhood—an inner renewal which is achieved as personal and racial unconscious forces become available to the person" (36).

The Brothers Grimm

Jacob Ludwig Carl Grimm (1785-1863) and Wilhelm Carl Grimm (1786-1859), known as the Brothers Grimm, were German folklorists. The fairy tales for which they became famous were published in the *Kinder und Hausmärchen* (1812-22). They claimed that their fairy tales came from oral sources, though a few were found in old manuscripts as part of their research.

Austrian Bettelheim, who heard fairy tales from his mother, vastly prefers the Grimm brothers' tales to those of other fabulists, such as Charles Perrault. He sees the Grimm Brothers as less aristocratic and more authentic and thus more helpful to children. For example, while Perrault makes Little Red Riding Hood's seduction by the wolf explicit, the Grimm Brothers leave it implicit, thus providing scope for the child to meet the tale at their stage in development and divine a personalized significance from it. Bettelheim admits that many of the Grimm Brothers' stories begin with Christian motifs; however, he overlooks this aspect to make their work more relevant to a secular age.

Charles Perrault

Charles Perrault (1628-1703) was a French courtier best known for his *Tales of Mother Goose* (1697). These included some of the most famous fairy tales such as "Cinderella" and "Sleeping Beauty." At the end of each tale, Perrault adds a moralistic verse, intended to instruct a child reader about the meaning of the tale.

Bettelheim often refers to Perrault's older versions of the stories before moving to a deeper analysis of the Grimm Brothers' adaptations. Bettelheim refers to Perrault as "the academician" and implies that he was sometimes impeded from getting to the bloody heart of the fairy tale by his courtly environment (228). For example, when Perrault dampens down Basile's Italian version of the Sleeping Beauty, in which "a married king ravishes a sleeping maiden" and "gets her with child" (229), Bettelheim considers that "this is not that Perrault was lacking in artistry, but that he did not take his fairy stories seriously and was most intent on the cute or moralistic verse ending he appended to each" (230).

Bettelheim also criticizes Perrault for destroying fairy tales' "feeling of timelessness" and universality by adding details that were specific to Perrault's time (230); for example, in the detail that the awakening Sleeping Beauty's costume was old-fashioned, in the style of "my great-grandmother, and had a point peeping over a high collar" (230). Bettelheim believes that such specificity makes the tale less useful; it impedes the child's ability to imagine what Sleeping Beauty looks like for themselves, and this hinders their identification with the heroine.

Themes

Defending the Fairy Tale's Violence

One of Bettelheim's key objectives in writing *The Uses of Enchantment* is to defend the fairy tale from modern educators who denounce it as too violent for young children. Instead, such moderns prefer tamer realistic narratives that, on the surface, appear to mirror an urban American 20th-century child's predicament more closely than a fairy tale set in a medieval-seeming European setting. For his part, Bettelheim finds such modern children's literature too "shallow in substance that little of significance can be gained" (4). Such stories, in Bettelheim's view, do not address a young child's developmental problems, and they leave children feeling alone with their darkest and scariest imaginings. These stories' wishful portrayal of a world where everyone is good seems untrue to children who "know that *they* are not always good" (7), and, being exposed to such literature exclusively, children risk becoming monsters to themselves. Conversely, fairy tales—which show young protagonists facing monsters and adults who want to destroy those protagonists prior to the happy ending—give the child reader a sense that they, like the protagonist, can cope with their most challenging problems.

Bettelheim remarks that the advent of psychoanalysis showed the truth about the destructive and sadistic nature of a child's imagination, whereby he "not only loves his parents with an incredible intensity of feeling, but at times also hates them" (120). While such an internal state mirrors the good mother and evil stepmother motif present in fairy tales, the fairy tale's detractors thought that the violence perpetrated between these malign adults and the child protagonists would be too much for a real child to handle. Such hatred is a disturbing fact for parents to contemplate, and it is at the root of their censorship of fairy tales. Bettelheim's response is that the child's anxieties and destructive urges will be present regardless of the parents' censorship. While the fairy tale gives the child's anxieties "form and body" (121) in addition to offering solutions (such as putting the tormenting witch in the oven and mastering her), a life without such tales forces the child to repress their fears in their unconscious. Without the fairy tale to show the child that their feelings are normal and common, the child may feel that they are uniquely bad for their violent impulses or rapacious appetites. A child feels safe and confident when they see the truth of their inner state mirrored in the tale. Additionally, the tale is set in a faraway, old-fashioned location; this distance enables the child to identify with the protagonist whilst at the same time remaining safe because they know that witches and ogres live in a land that is separate from their own.

Some parents also object to the medieval nature of the punishments dealt to fairy tales' evildoers. For example, the witch in "Hansel and Gretel" is shoved into the oven, while the evil queen in "Snow White" is made to dance to death in red-hot shoes. While parents may fear that such punishments will scar children, Bettelheim maintains that children gain a sense of completion from seeing evil be humiliated, destroyed, and removed from a sphere where it can harm the protagonist. For example, the punishment of dancing to death in burning shoes, inflicted on the evil queen in "Snow White," teaches the moral that "uncontrolled passion must be restrained or it will become one's undoing" and that "only the death of the jealous queen (the elimination of all outer and inner turbulence) can make for a happy world" (214). Here, Bettelheim argues that the child reaches catharsis through the queen's punishment, as they eliminate the jealous queen that rages rampant within them and identify with the ego-strengthened protagonist who is now rid of her.

Overall, Bettelheim contends that parents' objections to fairy tale violence arise from their own wishful fantasies of uncomplicated peaceful narratives and loving, untroubled children. Under this view, such parents are in denial regarding both the complicated nature of their children and their own parental inability to protect them from the real world. Instead, Bettelheim argues, they should accept their children for the complex beings they are and provide them with tools, like the fairy tale, that help them confront the harshest aspects in life.

The Happy Ending as Promised Land

Bettelheim continually posits that a happy ending is the child's reward for undergoing existential tribulations alongside the fairy tale protagonist. For Bettelheim, the happy ending is what differentiates the fairy tale from the myth and makes it "optimistic, no matter how terrifyingly serious some features of the story may be" (37). As the child identifies with the protagonist, the happy ending gives them hope for their own future. The vast majority of fairy tales Bettelheim selects have an unambiguously happy ending, and he judges those that do not—such as "Goldilocks and the Three Bears"—as being less useful to the child.

While Bettelheim considers that "Goldilocks and the Three Bears" deals with the important developmental problems of oedipal struggles and search for identity, as Goldilocks tries the different bears' porridge and furniture, the bears' indifference to her presence is problematic. At the end of the story, when Goldilocks jumps out of the window on the bears' return and "they act as if nothing had happened but an interlude without consequences," Bettelheim regards that such evasion symbolizes that "no solution of the oedipal predicaments or of sibling rivalry is necessary" (224). Bettelheim resents that Goldilocks' sojourn with the bears did not substantially change either of their lives and "despite her serious exploration of where she fits in—by implication, of who she is— we are not told that it led to any higher selfhood for Goldilocks" (224). Without the protagonist modeling clarity about one's identity and progression to the next stage of development, the happy ending is marred, and the child reader does not accrue "emotional maturity" (224). While Bettelheim states elsewhere in the book that fairy tales are works of art that work subconsciously and idiosyncratically in every child, his preference for a happy ending indicates the contradictory wish that stories should universally deliver reassurance and a sense of progression in the protagonists' psyche.

In his *New York Times* review, John Updike stated that "neither Bettelheim nor the fairy tales doubt that they know what happiness is." Both present happiness as a move towards independence and being ruler of one's own kingdom. Most of all, the happy ending reaches its apotheosis in marriage, "which alone can take the sting out of the narrow limits of our time on this earth: forming a truly satisfying bond to another" (10). From a psychoanalytic perspective, marriage also represents the completion of the psychosexual stages of development, as the protagonist enters their genital phase, whereby they are an active participant in the world. However, while in fairy tales marriage means a lifelong bond and permanent happiness, in the 1970s when Bettelheim was writing, the unhappy marriage was well publicized, and between a quarter and a third of marriages ended in divorce (Wilcox, W. Bradford. "The Evolution of Divorce." *National Affairs.* 2009). Moreover, feminist and gay liberation movements were beginning to propose alternative happy endings to heterosexual coupledom. Thus, while Bettelheim endorsed marriage as the happiest conclusion, his society was becoming disillusioned with the institution. For Updike, Bettelheim's emphasis on the happy ending weakened his argument, as the writer saw that the psychoanalyst's "enchanting presumption of life as a potentially successful adventure may be itself something of a fairy tale." Certainly, the happy ending would seem to be a fairy tale for Bettelheim himself, who saw his first marriage end and who died by suicide after being widowed from his second.

However, according to Bettelheim, the unrealistic nature of a fairy tale ending is irrelevant to a child's engagement with fairy tales. Bettelheim stipulates that at this early stage in human life, the most important thing is that the fairy tale's happy ending reassures the child that everything will be okay if they take the risky next step towards independence and autonomy. Thus, a five-year-old in the throes of oedipal and separation anxiety who reads about a happy marriage between a prince and a princess, learns that the happy ending is "not made possible, as the child wishes and believes, by holding onto his mother eternally" (11). Instead, the "true interpersonal relation" symbolized by the marriage bond reassures the child that if they risk independence and go out into the world, they will re-encounter the kind of love they received from their mother (11). Bettelheim argues that for the child at this stage in development, such reassurance is enough to help them rely less upon their mother and look more towards their peers. When a parent tells a child a fairy tale, they encourage the child's belief that independence will bring about a happy ending; the child gains the added reassurance that their parent believes in their ability to find happiness apart from them. Overall, then, the happy ending in fairy tales is less about the actual events of a life and more about the child's capacity to confidently progress to the next stage in development.

Gender and the Interpretation of Fairy Tales

Bettelheim's attitude to gender is contradictory. On the one hand, he stresses that all children can derive a personalized meaning from all fairy tales, regardless of the gender of the protagonist. For example, he shows how "Rapunzel," a fairy tale in which the adolescent protagonist uses her long tresses to defy the sorceress and see her prince, was a favorite of both a seven-year-old girl and a five-year-old boy. The girl, who had suffered the loss of her biological mother and saw her father remarry, made an obvious identification with Rapunzel as "her stepmother was clearly the witch of the story, and she was the girl locked away in the tower" (131). Bettelheim adds that the girl's sense of powerlessness also fed into the identification: The "'witch had forcibly' obtained" Rapunzel, "as her stepmother had forcibly worked her way into the girl's life" (131). "Rapunzel" thus consoled the girl given that it reinforced her sense of autonomy and promoted the hopeful idea that a prince would come and rescue her from the situation.

While the girl's experience in many ways paralleled Rapunzel's and caused her to receive the most obvious form of consolation from the story, there was then the five-year-old boy from a single-parent family who was feeling insecure owing to his mother and grandmother's temporary absences. This boy derived a unique meaning from the story. The elements that were important to him were the security of the tower in which the substitute mother (the sorceress) keeps Rapunzel, and the fact that Rapunzel could escape the situation through her muscular tresses, representing the strength of her own body. For the boy, "that one's body can provide a lifeline reassured him that, if necessary, he would similarly find in his own body the source of his security" (17). Thus, when the boy's main caretaker, his grandmother, was hospitalized, he derived consolation from the tale's idea that he could rely on his own body to stay safe and grow up. Bettelheim concludes that the imagery and symbolism in the fairy tale has fluid and indirect applications and so can "have much to offer to a little boy even if the story's heroine is an adolescent girl" (17). He implies that it is up to the child to derive meaning from the tale and they will do so in ways that are more creative and unpredictable than simply comparing their lives to those of the fairy tale protagonist. Still, there is some gender anxiety on Bettelheim's part, as he seeks to reassure parents that this often-feminized form of literature will not emasculate their sons.

Even as Bettelheim argues that fairy tales about female protagonists can aid the development of young boys and so encourage empathy between the genders, he has the patriarchal tendency to portray the default child as male. This is obvious in his outdated use of the masculine pronoun "he" to refer to a theoretical, generalized child. While this practice reflects the academic style of the early 20th century, by the 1970s it had come under criticism by feminists for diminishing female subjectivity and experience.

Moreover, Bettelheim's interpretations of female-centered fairy tales often reinforce harmful and limiting stereotypes about girls and women. He is not critical of the social and cultural contexts from which fairy tales arose or about their retrogressive messages about femininity and female fulfillment. This is evident in his discussion of the stepsisters in "Cinderella." He makes clear that Cinderella, with her small feet, is the most desirable of the sisters, as her smallness contrasts with the largeness ascribed to males and is "especially feminine" (268). He writes that "to have such big feet that they don't fit the slipper makes the stepsisters more masculine than Cinderella—therefore less desirable" (268). In order to fit the prescribed standard of feminine perfection, the sisters engage in "symbolic self-castration to prove their femininity" when they mutilate their feet in order to fit the slipper (268). Here, the stereotype of worthy, honest women like Cinderella, who are already perfect and only must be themselves to be desirable, is set against the stereotype of inadequate, dishonest women who deceive in order to fit an ideal. While Bettelheim believes that the child reader will identify with Cinderella, the stepsisters' measures to become acceptable represent the bodily modifications women have perennially made in order to be more feminine and make men secure about their position. Some readers may therefore relate more to the sisters (and the culture that produced their anxieties) than to Cinderella's good fortune. As these stepsisters do not fulfill the expectations of their gender, they do not meet a happy ending. While one could make the argument that the destruction of the stepsisters represents a destruction of vanity and deceit in the child's psyche, the sisters being judged as lesser and unfeminine, based on patriarchal standards of bodily perfection, conveys a harmful message to young girls.

Although Bettelheim asserts that fairy tales can be interpreted in manifold ways and can serve children of both genders, his neglect of these tales' patriarchal cultural and historical context limits his ability to sincerely affirm young girls' identity. Instead, in Bettelheim's interpretations, as in the tales themselves, girls are taught that they must form their identity within patriarchal expectations.

Index of Terms

Fairy Tale

The fairy tales discussed by Bettelheim generally feature child or adolescent protagonists; a magical or supernatural element; and a bucolic European, or in some cases, Arabian setting that is far removed from urban 20th-century America in which the author was writing. While the fairy tales were collected and given written form by writers such as the Brothers Grimm or Charles Perrault, they stem from an oral tradition and often collect generations' worth of stories and wisdom. Significantly, Bettelheim mentions the dominant female role of mothers like his own and that of the German poet Goethe in telling the fairy tales. Bettelheim encourages parents to become part of the oral tradition in telling the tales to their children rather than encouraging the children to independently discover the works. The tale can thus connect parent and child, even as its contents reveal the violent impulses children have towards their parents and vice versa.

While fairy tales, like myths, make use of the supernatural, fairy tales differ from myths in the mundanity of their settings. Their protagonists are not "absolutely unique" either by birth or ability; they are relatable characters who learn to make the best of the opportunities presented to them (37). While the mythic heroes fulfill all of the superego's demands, fairy tale protagonists learn to use their superego and ego to master the id and achieve an integrated personality. This is important for the child's ability to identify with the characters and hold them as an inspiration for their own happy future. Bettelheim also posits that fairy tales differ from myths in having a happy ending rather than a tragic one. The fairy tale's optimism also makes it a more encouraging story for a child, who is assured that their labors in growing up will bear fruit.

Integrated Personality

As a Freudian psychoanalyst, Bettelheim viewed that the human personality was made up of three components: the unconscious, animalistic id, driven by appetites for food, sex, and violence; the ego, the conscious part of ourselves that makes rational decisions and is the version we present to the world; and the superego, the moral conscience that influences the ego and is made up of parental and societal values.

While all three components are present in all humans, mature adults are better capable of bringing the id under the control of the ego and superego and even channeling it as their life force. In contrast, young children, who have not resolved their oedipal conflicts, can often find themselves overwhelmed by the id.

For Bettelheim, fairy tales help children to see and integrate the different parts of their personality because these stories give free rein to the id. The id in fairy tales can arrive in the form of a murderous stepmother, a man-eating giant, or a lustful Bluebeard figure who rapes and murders girls. Such extreme manifestations of the id may intimidate parents, but these figures recognize and give symbolic form to a child's most basic impulses. By allowing children to identify with the hero and gain ego-strength through them, the fairy tale encourages children to defeat their base impulses and move on to the next stage in development.

However, when it comes to the Animal Groom cycle of fairy tales, Bettelheim emphasizes the importance of befriending and valuing "animal nature"; in order to achieve happy marriage, says Bettelheim, heroines must address the repression that causes them to view sexuality as bestial (78). By thus valuing the animal nature of their grooms, the fairy tale heroines socialize the id and can contemplate the former taboo of sexuality as a natural part of life.

Oedipus Complex

The Oedipus complex refers to the Freudian psychoanalytic concept that children aged three to five are attracted to their opposite-sex parent and see the same-sex parent as competition. The complex refers to the original Greek myth where Oedipus kills his father and marries his mother. In young children, it manifests in fantasies of wanting to get the same-sex parent out of the way so that they can enjoy all of the opposite-sex parent's attention. This then becomes fraught with the anxiety that the same-sex parent will find out, seek to destroy them, and succeed because they are much stronger.

Bettelheim argues that fairy tales offer models for recognizing and renegotiating the Oedipus complex; for example, he conjectures that the evil stepmother in "Snow White," who seeks to kill Snow White repeatedly, functions as a daughter's projection that because she is jealous of the attention her mother receives from her father, her mother must be jealous of her. In such a reversal, "the feeling of inferiority is defensively turned into a feeling of superiority" (204). While the tale illustrates Snow White's oedipal anxieties, it shows how, through a process of maturation, her immature and potentially incestuous love for her father is transferred onto her rescuing prince. Thus, says Bettelheim, fairy tales offer the consolation that although one will lose out to the same-sex parent in the oedipal battle, they will be rewarded with a partner who will make them the center of their attention.

Stages of Psychosexual Development: Oral, Anal, Phallic, Latent, and Genital

Invoking a Freudian concept of childhood development, Bettelheim reminds parents that the passage from infancy to adulthood is neither smooth nor automatic. Instead, a child passes through successive stages of development, each of which must give way to a more mature stage. Fairy tales illustrate these transitions in symbolic form.

The oral stage in development characterizes a child's experience from birth to about 18 months. During this time, the mouth is the chief pleasure organ, and the child is obsessed with filling it with food and other objects. As this stage of development coincides with breastfeeding, the mother is an all-providing nurturer and the child her receptacle. While no fairy tale protagonists are babies, some child heroes show evidence of inhabiting or regressing to an oral stage. For example, Jack in "Jack and the Beanstalk" experiences something that is akin to the end of the oral stage when his "good cow Milky White, who provided all that was needed, suddenly stops giving milk" (188). This "arouses dim memories" in the child "of that tragic time when the flow of milk ceased [...] when he was weaned" and "the mother demands that the child must learn to make do with what the outside world can offer" (188). For Jack, as for Hansel and Gretel, the end of the oral stage is symbolized by their parents' sending them out to make their own way. The fairy tales teach that a return to a previous stage is not possible and that the only way is forward. While modern children may be lucky enough not to be thrown out by their parents, they will unconsciously recognize fairy tale motifs that symbolize an end to the oral stage.

Still, the fairy tales also teach that the experience and memory of the all-giving mother of the oral stage is essential for child's belief in their ability to acquire satisfaction and happiness. According to Bettelheim, a key motivation in going out in the world is re-encountering "the all-giving mother of our infancy" in another form, as "preconsciously or unconsciously, it is this hope of finding her somewhere which gives us the strength to leave home" (94). The separation of the all-giving good mother from the demanding stepmother figure who replaces her allows the child to hold onto their good object and find confidence in their future.

Anal Stage of Development

In Freud's model of psychosocial development, the anal stage occurs between the ages of one and three. It coincides with potty training and results in the child's fascination with its own processes of elimination. The anal stage is important for a child's later ability to be clean and orderly. Bettelheim does not explore this stage in development in his study of fairy tales, only once mentioning that Jack's hoarding of the bag of gold and golden eggs "stand for anal ideas of possession" (193). Jack's eventual preference of the golden harp, an instrument that he can show off as it facilitates his entry into the social world, indicates that he will now progress to the phallic stage.

Phallic Stage of Development

The phallic stage in development occurs between the ages of three and six when the child transfers their attention to their genitals. This consolation for the distance between the child and their increasingly demanding parent arrives in the form of "a fantastically exaggerated belief in what his body and his organs will do for him" (189). The child sees sexuality as "something that he can achieve all by himself" (189). While this is not the ultimate stage in maturity, such "(unrealistic) belief in himself" enables the child to meet the world and its challenges (189). In "Jack and the Beanstalk," the incipient phallic stage enables Jack to give up his regressive oral fixation on the cow, in exchange for the seeds that would grant him autonomy. The huge resulting beanstalk symbolizes Jack's "belief in magic phallic powers" (189). Eventually, fairy tale protagonists learn that such a belief in magic and the extraordinary power of the body becomes dissatisfying.

Latent and Genital stages follow the phallic stage of development; however, Bettelheim does not discuss these. The latent stage, which occurs from about age six and the onset of puberty, is when the child's libido is dormant or sublimated in platonic friendship or childish pastimes. Bettelheim states that Snow White's sojourn with the dwarves, with whom she has an entirely platonic relationship, is an example of her staying in the latency stage. The genital stage, which returns with puberty, is the final stage of psychosexual development and, for Freudian psychoanalysts, finds its expression in heterosexual intercourse. Although Bettelheim states that fairy tale protagonists enter this stage when they are ripe to make happy marriages, he does not explicitly discuss it. One can infer that in his discussion of the Animal Groom cycle of tales, the heroines must seek to end the latent period, which has repressed their sexuality, by integrating the different parts of their personality and progressing to the genital stage.

Important Quotes

1. "To enrich his life, it must stimulate his imagination; help him to develop his intellect and to clarify his emotions; be attuned to his anxieties and aspirations; give full recognition to his difficulties, while at the same time suggesting solutions to the problems which perturb him. In short, it must at one and the same time relate to all aspects of his personality—and this without ever belittling, but, on the contrary, giving full credence to the seriousness of the child's predicaments, while simultaneously promoting confidence in himself and in his future."
(Introduction, Page 5)

Bettelheim sets out his specification for the ideal children's story. Overall, children's literature should be in touch with the imagination and anxieties of its target audience. The emphasis on giving "full recognition" to difficulties and appealing to "all aspects of his personality" indicates Bettelheim's view that children's literature should not offer anodyne depictions of a child's torments. Taboos brought up in the fairy tale will be compensated by the happy ending, as the child uses the story to generate solutions to their own problems. The fairy tale thus enables the child to face problems rather than escape them.

2. "When unconscious material *is* to some degree permitted to come to awareness and worked through in imagination, its potential for causing harm—to ourselves or others—is much reduced; some of its forces can then be made to serve positive purposes."
(Introduction, Page 7)

Bettelheim overturns the contemporary trend of trying to protect children from the worst of human experience; he argues that it is essential for children to address their taboos. When taboos appear in the imaginative form of literature, they can be safely worked through; whereas if they are repressed, they have more potential to cause harm. In stating that the "forces" of the unconscious can be useful, Bettelheim also encourages the controlling parent to not fear this more obscure side to their child.

3. "The figures in fairy tales are not ambivalent—not good and bad at the same time, as we all are in reality. But since polarization dominates the child's mind, it also dominates fairy tales. [...] Presenting the polarities of

character permits the child to comprehend easily the difference between the two, which he could not do as readily were the figures drawn more true to life, with all the complexities that characterize real people. Ambiguities must wait until a relatively firm personality has been established on the basis of positive identifications."
(Introduction, Page 9)

The polarities of good and bad in fairy tales suit a young child's grasp of reality. Bettelheim argues that unrealistically good or bad characters are helpful, as the child with their personality in flux is looking for someone with whom to identify. Later, when the child has made enough positive identifications, they are more ready to cope with ambiguous characters.

4. "Only a small number of fairy tales are widely known. Most of the points made in this book could have been illustrated more vividly if some of the more obscure fairy stories could have been referred to. But since these tales, though once familiar, are presently unknown, it would have been necessary to reprint them here, making for a book of unwieldy size."
(Introduction, Page 14)

Bettelheim's reference to the loss of fairy tales underscores their fragility and value. By stating that the most obscure tales could perhaps be the most useful, Bettelheim suggests that some of the most precious examples have been lost. As a tool of persuasion, this theoretically creates nostalgia in the reader and supports Bettelheim's campaign in rescuing the fairy tale from oblivion.

5. "Fairy tales have great psychological meaning for children of all ages, both boys and girls, irrespective of the age and sex of the story's hero. Rich personal meaning is gained from fairy stories because they facilitate changes in identification as the child deals with different problems, one at a time."
(Introduction, Page 17)

Here, Bettelheim makes the crucial point that, in the process of making identifications, children are often more sophisticated than their parents think they are. Thus, two very different children at different stages of development will each derive a highly specific, individual meaning from the same tale. In emphasizing that the child will deal with their problems one at a time, Bettelheim acknowledges the slow nature of child development.

6. "The fairy tale is therapeutic because the patient finds his *own* solutions, through contemplating what the story seems to imply about him and his inner conflicts at this moment in his life. The content of the chosen tale usually has nothing to do with the patient's external life, but much to do with his inner problems, which seem incomprehensible and hence unsolvable."
(Part 1, Page 25)

Here, Bettelheim emphasizes the active nature of the fairy tale, whereby the Hindu patient subconsciously applies the story to their inner life. While the problems previously seemed beyond the patient, the tale may help them reorganize their internal world and find their own creative solutions for what keeps them stuck. Thus, by contemplating heroes, the patient learns to be the hero of their own story.

7. "To the child, the parent's absence seems an eternity—a feeling that remains unaffected by Mother's truthful explanation that she was gone for only half an hour. So the fairy tale's fantastic exaggeration gives it the ring of psychological truth—while realistic explanations seem psychologically untrue, however true to fact."
(Part 1, Page 32)

Bettelheim shows how the fairy tales' untruths, such as exaggerated timescales that deal with eternity, are closer to the child's inner experience of truth than are empirical realities. This means that the fairy tale has a unique appeal to the child because it addresses how they already see the world; whereas the realistic narrative falls short on truth despite its mission to accurately portray reality.

8. "The fairy tale [...] is very much the result of common conscious and unconscious content having been shaped by the conscious mind, not of one particular person, but the consensus of many in regard to what they view as universal human problems, and what they accept as desirable solutions."
(Part 1, Page 36)

Here, Bettelheim illustrates the unique power of the fairy tale, in being a collection of manifold consciousnesses over time rather than the work of one particular author. This gives power to the fairy tale's notions of good and evil, as they have been formed by multiple generations over time. Bettelheim presents fairy tale morality as a universal without judging that its attitudes to have been shaped by centuries of European culture.

9. "Life on a small planet surrounded by limitless space seems awfully lonely and cold to a child—just the opposite of what he knows life ought to be. This is why the ancients needed to feel sheltered and warmed by an enveloping mother figure. To depreciate protective imagery like this as mere childish projections of an immature mind is to rob the young child of one aspect of the prolonged safety and comfort he needs."
(Part 1, Page 50)

Bettelheim wrote during the early period of space exploration, when research increasingly showed the smallness of earth in comparison to the entire universe. He argues that coming to terms with this bleak reality and one's own insignificance in the world ought to be the province of a developed, rational mind. A child's mind, in contrast, may be harmed by such a stark presentation of reality. The "protective imagery" of fairy tales, however, provides a period of prolonged safety that will enable the child to deal with the real world. Still, while Bettelheim advocates a child's exposure to the reality of feelings, no matter how intense, he also advises delaying a child's discovery of scientific facts that diminish their place in the universe.

10. "Fairy tales offer figures onto which the child can externalize what goes on in his mind, in controllable ways. Fairy tales show the child how he can embody his destructive wishes in one figure, gain desired satisfactions from another, identify with a third, have ideal attachments with a fourth, and so on, as his needs of the moment require."
(Part 1, Page 65)

Bettelheim illustrates how polarizing figures in fairy tale worlds can help the overwhelmed child negotiate their chaotic inner life and process their most destructive feelings. By creating a figure onto whom the child can channel these emotions, a fairy tale prevents overwhelm and provides space for other aspects of the child's consciousness. Additionally, Bettelheim's idea that the child will "identify with a third" embodies his belief that the child is always third in a fairy story, as figures one and two signal the child's parents. Again, he emphasizes that the fairy tale is adaptable and services the child's particular needs in the moment.

11. "A small child can do little on his own, and this is disappointing to him—so much so that he may give up in despair. The fairy story prevents this by giving extraordinary dignity to the smallest achievements, and suggesting that the most wonderful consequences may grow out of it."
(Part 1, Page 73)

Bettelheim shows how the fairy story adapts itself to a child's perception of the world. Far from trivializing a child's small gestures towards independence, the fairy tale celebrates and encourages these efforts. The story thus gives the child faith that every developmental step is important and that everyday achievements can lead to a marvelous future of autonomy.

12. "Given the contradictory tendencies residing within me, which of them should I respond to? The fairy-tale answer is the same one which psychoanalysis offers: To avoid being tossed about and, in extreme cases torn apart by our ambivalences requires that we integrate them. Only in this way can we achieve a unified personality able to meet successfully, with inner security, the difficulties of living."
(Part 1, Page 89)

Bettelheim asserts that the integration of our contradictory tendencies is essential to personal growth. He parallels the fairy tale's use of moralistic and animalistic personalities with psychoanalysis' reference to the superego and the id. While one is in judgment of the other, we will be riven with conflict. However, the fairy tale offers many examples of how the two can live in harmony, as a superego-dominated character exerts power and influence over an id-dominated one.

13. "The unconscious is the source of raw materials and the basis upon which the ego erects the edifice of our personality. In this simile our fantasies are the natural resources which provide and shape this raw material, making it useful for the ego's personality-building tasks. If we are deprived of this natural resource, our life remains limited; without fantasies to give us hope, we do not have the strength to meet the adversities of life. Childhood is the time when these fantasies need to be nurtured."
(Part 1, Page 121)

Bettelheim argues that far from being frivolous, fantasy enables children to imagine and build a future-orientated ego. Without fantasy, a child will only attain limited development, and they will be ill-equipped to meet challenges. This is arguably because they have not practiced imagining themselves as more creative and capable than they are at present, and thus future challenges will seem insurmountable.

14. "Listening to a fairy tale and taking in the images it presents may be

compared to a scattering of seeds, only some of which will be implanted in the mind of the child. Some of these will be working in his conscious mind right away; others will stimulate processes in the unconscious. [...] But those seeds which have fallen on the right soil will grow into beautiful flowers and sturdy trees—that is, give validity to important feelings, promote insights, nourish hopes, reduce anxieties—and in doing so enrich the child's life at the moment and forever after."
(Part 1, Page 154)

By using the metaphor of seeds and plants, Bettelheim conveys the tale's organic effect on the child's conscience. Through the image of germination in dark soil, Bettelheim alerts the parent that the fairy tale is having an effect beyond the immediate moment. As the story takes root in the child's unconscious, time will pass before results appear.

15. "Fairy tales speak to our conscious and unconscious, and therefore do not need to avoid contradictions, since these easily coexist in our unconscious."
(Part 2, Page 174)

Bettelheim argues that the contradictions in fairy tales are consonant with those of the human unconscious. While the conscious human wishes to avoid contradictions to make life simpler, the fairy tale is wiser in allowing the conflicting psychic elements to coexist.

16. "Giving up oral dependency is acceptable only if the child can find security in a realistic—or more likely, a fantastically exaggerated—belief in what his body and its organs will do for him. But a child sees in sexuality not something based on a relation between a man and a woman, but something that he can achieve all by himself."
(Part 2, Page 189)

Bettelheim explains how the phallic stage of development displaces the primary oral stage as Jack gives up hope that his mother will be the supreme provider and begins to rely on himself and the apparent magic within his increasingly capable body. While the phallic stage is not the ultimate stage of development, Bettelheim shows how a child's progression towards adulthood is evolutionary, as one less immature stage succeeds another. The adult reader, who realizes that nothing in life can be achieved on one's own, knows that Jack has not reached the apex of maturity.

17. "The magic mirror seems to speak with the voice of a daughter rather than that of a mother. As the small girl thinks her mother is the most beautiful person in the world, this is what the mirror initially tells the queen. But as the older girl thinks she is much more beautiful than her mother, this is what the mirror says later. [...] The mirror says: 'She is a thousand times more beautiful'—a statement much more akin to an adolescent's exaggeration which he makes to enlarge his advantages and silence his inner voice of doubt."
(Part 2, Page 207)

Bettelheim offers the fresh argument that the famous magic mirror in "Snow White" speaks in the voice of the daughter who takes her mother as a role-model but, as she grows, seeks to surpass her in beauty and influence. The exaggeration on the daughter's part demonstrates how she uses her fantasy to overcome her mother by imagining herself as superior. Such boldness is needed to erase the terrifying doubt that the mother may always be the more powerful and the daughter's existence superfluous.

18. "The number three is central in 'Goldilocks' [...] it relates to [...] finding out who one is biologically. Three also stands for the relations within the nuclear family, and efforts to ascertain where one fits in there. Thus, three symbolizes a search for who one is biologically (sexually), and who one is in relation to the most important persons in one's life."
(Part 2, Page 220)

Bettelheim claims the precedence of the number three in "Goldilocks" is not incidental. The number of bears—and subsequent number of chairs, beds, and bowls of porridge—represents the "nuclear family" of two parents and a child. Goldilocks oscillates between the three positions in her attempt to discover her role in the family setup. This role relates to her identity.

19. "What may seem like a period of deathlike passivity at the end of childhood is nothing but a time of quiet growth and preparation, from which the person will awaken mature, ready for sexual union. It must be stressed that in fairy tales this union is as much one of the minds and souls of two partners as it is one of sexual fulfillment."
(Part 2, Page 232)

Bettelheim argues that the extraordinary hundred-year sleep in "The Sleeping Beauty" has a parallel in adolescent development. In a comparison to the Beauty's sleep, he cites the recognizable introversion that affects many adolescents, where the child turns away from the world to be better able to face it as a mature person. For Bettelheim, as for the fairy tale, the epitome of maturity is characterized by union with a partner. While, on a literal level, this refers to sex and marriage, on a metaphorical level, the ability to unite with other bodies and souls indicates a readiness to actively engage with the world.

20. "One of the greatest merits of 'Cinderella' is that, irrespective of the magic help Cinderella receives, the child understands that essentially it is through her own efforts, and because of the person she is, that Cinderella is able to transcend magnificently her degraded state, despite what appear as insurmountable obstacles. It gives the child confidence that the same will be true for him, because the story relates to his conscious and his unconscious guilt."
(Part 2, Page 243)

Bettelheim posits that despite the magical nature of fairy tales, they enable children to understand that the protagonists triumph because of their character and not because of magical assistance. As the child has none of the magical tools available to Cinderella but believes themself capable of having her character, her story is still encouraging for them. Bettelheim also believes that because the tale addresses the child's guilt about wanting to eliminate or punish their parents, the child's positive identification with the protagonist has deep roots.

21. "It seems as if these stories deliberately avoid stating that the heroines are in love; one gets the impression that even fairy tales put little stock in love at first sight. Instead, they suggest that much more is involved in loving than being awakened or chosen by some prince."
(Part 2, Page 277)

Bettelheim here references the bashfulness of heroines such as Snow White and Sleeping Beauty towards their rescuing princes, as the tales elaborate little on their feelings. Thus, in those fairy tales, the components of being "in love" remain mysterious, especially on the feminine part. While, in the cultural imagination, fairy tales seem to embody the stereotype of love at first sight, the truth is more complicated. Rather than love happening automatically, the heroine must reach a new stage of developmental maturity before she can fall in love.

22. "Fairy tales suggest that eventually there comes a time when we

must learn what we have not known before—or, to put it psychoanalytically, to undo the repression of sex. What we had experienced as dangerous, loathsome, something to be shunned, must change its appearance so that it is experienced as truly beautiful. It is love which permits this to happen."
(Part 2, Page 279)

In his introduction to the animal groom cycle of fairy tales, Bettelheim prepares the reader for a group of stories that depict the transformation of sexual repression through the sublimating feeling of love. The magic lies in the fact that something formerly loathsome acquires beauty, while the development in the hero or heroine occurs when they rediscover, in a new light, what they previously termed as animalistic.

23. "We do not learn why the groom was forced to take on the form of an ugly animal, or why this harm inflicted on him remains unpunished. This suggests that the change from the 'natural' or beautiful appearance took place in the unfathomable past when we did not know why something happened to us, even when it had the most far-reaching consequences. Shall we say that the repression of sex occurred so early that it cannot be recalled? None of us remember at what moment in our life sex first took on the form of something animal-like."
(Part 2, Page 283)

Bettelheim argues that the mystery of why the groom was transformed into an animal in fairy tales parallels our own confusion about when sex became repressed in our own psyches. The "unfathomable past" refers to a time before our conscious memories and is thus inaccessible. However, the fairy tale's ambiguity about this transformation-repression allows us to contemplate that a similar process may have occurred in us.

24. "Our oedipal attachments, far from being only the source of our greatest emotional difficulties (which they can be when they do not undergo proper development during our growing up), are the soil out of which permanent happiness grows if we experience the right evolution and resolution of these feelings."
(Part 2, Page 307)

In explaining how Beauty's extended attachment to her father transforms into a more mature love for the Beast, Bettelheim demonstrates how Beauty's earlier immature love already contained the seeds of the one that would ensure her future happiness. The metaphor of fertile soil indicates the basic primary materials for creating something visibly beautiful in the future. Thus, says Bettelheim, as long as the early oedipal attachments evolve and are redirected, they become a precondition of marital felicity. Bettelheim's idealistic vision of permanent happiness mirrors the attitude at the end of fairy tales.

25. "Each fairy tale is a magic mirror which reflects some aspects of our inner world, and of the steps required by our evolution from immaturity to maturity. For those who immerse themselves in what the fairy tale has to communicate, it becomes a deep, quiet pool which at first seems to reflect only our own image; but behind it we soon discover the inner turmoils of our soul—its depth and ways to gain peace within ourselves and the world, which is the reward of our struggles."
(Part 2, Page 309)

Bettelheim uses the fairy tale image of a magic mirror, which reflects more than the present reality, to show the story's more important ability to reflect realities beneath the surface: The turmoils it reflects are those within us, as we progress stage by stage from immaturity to maturity. The peace we gain aligns with the essentially optimistic nature of the fairy tale, as we feel that we can face our struggles and, at the same time, be promised a happy ending.

Essay Topics

1. In Bettelheim's view, how might readers of different genders respond to fairy tales? To what extent do you agree with his opinion?

2. What is the significance of the Animal Groom cycle of fairy tales? How do these stories help children and adolescents negotiate their relationship to sexuality?

3. In your opinion and with close reference to the text, why is a fairy tale's ending so important? Do you think that the happy endings of fairy tales are unhelpfully unrealistic or an important part of encouraging child confidence?

4. What is the significance of the vague and faraway settings of fairy tales? How does this aid a child's ability to derive meaning from their themes?

5. Why does Bettelheim prefer the fairy tale to modern, realistic types of children's literature? Why does he consider the latter's lack of violence to be a problem?

6. According to Bettelheim, why is the moral polarization of characters an important aspect of the fairy tale? Why is it especially important for a child to split the mother figure into an all-giving good mother and a wicked stepmother?

7. How do fairy tales help children progress in psychosexual development? Refer to at least two tales in your answer.

8. . What is fairy tales' role in personality integration? Why does

Bettelheim praise fairy tales for giving full license to the id?

9. Why does Bettelheim believe that a rich imaginative life is important for a young child, and how do fairy tales help in this respect? Refer to at least two tales in your answer.

10. How does Bettelheim counter the modern objections to fairy tales? To what extent do you agree with his view that fairy tales are perennially important for young children?

Printed in Great Britain
by Amazon

77087345R00041